D1570929

Management Lessons from Taiichi Ohno

Management Lessons from Taiichi Ohno

What Every Leader Can Learn from the Man Who Invented THE TOYOTA PRODUCTION SYSTEM

TAKEHIKO HARADA

New York   Chicago   San Francisco   Athens   London
Madrid   Mexico City   Milan   New Delhi
Singapore   Sydney   Toronto

This title was originally published in Japan with this original copyright notice:
MONO NO NAGARE WO TSUKURU HITO
OHNO TAIICHI-SAN GA TSUTAETAKATTA TOP KANRISHA NO YAKUWARI
Copyright © 2013 by Takehiko Harada
English translation rights arranged with THE NIKKAN KOGYO SHINBUN, LTD. through Japan UNI Agency, Inc.

1 2 3 4 5 6 7 8 9 0   DOC/DOC   1 2 1 0 9 8 7 6 5

ISBN   978-0-07-184973-9
MHID   0-07-184973-4

e-ISBN   978-0-07-184974-6
e-MHID   0-07-184974-2

Library of Congress Cataloging-in-Publication Data

Harada, Takehiko.
    Management lessons from Taiichi Ohno : what every leader can learn from the man who invented the Toyota production system / Takehiko Harada.
        pages cm
    ISBN 978-0-07-184973-9 (alk. paper)
    ISBN 0-07-184973-4 (alk. paper)
    1. Ono, Taiichi, 1912-1990. 2. Toyota Jidosha Kabushiki Kaisha—Management. 3. Leadership. 4. Management. I. Title.
    HD9710.J34T64524 2015
    658.4'092—dc23   2015009596

CONTENTS

CHAPTER 2   The Role of the Top

CHAPTER 3   The Role of Management: Enable Your Employees to Do the Work Well

CHAPTER 4   If You Respect Other People, They Will Trust You

TRANSLATOR'S NOTES AND INSIGHTS

Many times managers ask, "How can we sustain Lean?" This book points out the need to adopt a management mindset throughout the organization, starting with management. It provides anecdotes and practical steps to ensure that both the mindset and the purpose behind well-known techniques associated with the Toyota Production System (TPS) are understood and considered during implementation.

A number of books have been written about Ohno. Anecdotes such as being told to stand in one spot, fast changeovers, and the like are plentiful. His style of management could be considered dictatorial and bombastic, but beyond the mannerisms, there are basic, overarching principles that we find very useful.

By his strength of character, Ohno demonstrates the role that the leader must play at every level of management. Integrity, example/coaching, engagement at the floor level, risk taking and willingness to experiment to find better ways, and never being defensive about confronting problems are characteristics that can be found throughout the book. Neither providing solutions nor telling people what to do was his mode of operation. But he was never shy about confronting reality. He demonstrated that the people at the grassroots level have the capability to arrive at solutions.

This book was originally written for a Japanese audience, so it is written from a Japanese viewpoint. I have translated it the way it was written to keep the integrity of the book, and I have been careful not to edit things into or out of the original text. However, on occasion, I have added my own comments or clarifications as a Lean consultant who is living in Japan and has worked in many other countries as well. Hopefully, the comments will help drive home the truth that is written in this book, a truth that we can all use.

When I was first approached to translate this book, it started out as more of doing a favor for a friend. Once I met Mr. Harada, however, I knew that I wanted to dig deeper into what he was trying to say. Conversations with a Toyota manager that included "I hate stopwatches" and "Let them have as much inventory as they want" were intriguing, to say the least. As I started translating the book and started the e-mail flow between Takehiko and myself on concepts or the historical background to what he was saying, many things started to make sense. I realized that I had in fact picked up "fake Lean" concepts that I had had a problem with emotionally, but that I had never really had them articulated the way Harada explained them.

Looking back, I have to say that translating this book has been a sheer pleasure. The amount of time I spent on it, along with my many meetings and conversations with Mr. Harada, have truly been educational, and I have so appreciated Mr. Harada's willingness to spend his time with me and to discuss in detail the stories behind the episodes and the principles embedded in them.

Some of the areas that I had problems with were phrases like, "In the West, they don't care," or, "In Japan, we think differently." While I translated what was written word for word, it was sad to see that our Western culture is seen as "selfish" and "money before people"—both concepts that are viewed with contempt in Japan. This, unfortunately, looks more and more true for those companies that are doing Lean "just for the numbers." The phrase "profit comes after focusing on flow," which can be translated as "profit is a left-over after pursuing flow," really has deep meaning.

Personally, one of the greatest gems or confirmations for me in translating this book has been the absolute confirmation that biblical values are totally in line with what makes logical sense in creating a vibrant workplace. I had always known this intrinsically, but now I had authoritative backing. I think readers who grew up with values such as "do the right thing" or "love your neighbor as yourself," but then find that the workplace they are thrust into is not living these values, can take heart. It is possible.

Over the years, I've become a true believer that the results of Lean always need to be both better numbers and more smiles. Mr. Harada has certainly underlined that concept with this book, and on behalf of the whole Lean community, I thank him for it.

INTRODUCTION

n 1945, World War II had ended, and Japan was spent: spent of people, of money, of equipment, and even somewhat of spirit. At that time, a man by the name of Taiichi Ohno was promoted to manager of Toyota Motors' machine plant. Although everyone in his section opposed him, he came up with what at the time was an incomprehensible productivity improvement plan that challenged people with slogans like, "Limit the waste of overproduction and make only what is needed" and "Use fewer people," and that ended up delivering breakthrough productivity improvements.

What that involved was machines that used the jidoka concept: they didn't create defects or send them to the next process. They "stopped with an abnormality," and when the machines were on auto-cycle, people did other work. This concept was called "separating man from machine work." Laying out the processes from raw materials to finished goods in a one-piece-flow process sequence layout so that people flow and material flow happened allowed the company to make the necessary products with many fewer people than before.

When the "flow line" concept was coming into being, as Ohno was trying to limit overproduction, he took a hint from

U.S. supermarkets and came up with the concept that the downstream process comes and takes what it needs when it needs it—now known as downstream pull. This was in the late 1940s, and it was exactly the opposite of the normal way of operating, or transporting what was finished to the next process.

Ohno named the slip to buy parts the "withdrawal kanban," and named the slip to start production after the parts were taken away the "production kanban." The kanban system that allows for just-in-time production was born this way.

Since that time, whenever and wherever Taiichi Ohno's influence and responsibilities expanded, the implementation of flow and pull followed. Getting all the processes—raw materials and parts machining, and subassembly, and subassembly and the main assembly line—joined by downstream pull in a chain of withdrawal kanbans and production kanbans took him until the mid-1970s. This huge task took around 30 years!

This was the result of long years, many employees' hard work and hardship, and people racking their brains trying to come up with the best method of moving forward. The reason this approach succeeded was because of Mr. Taiichi Ohno's strong leadership and his stubborn persistent refusal to compromise on attaining the ideal. I believe that at the core, what drove Ohno was his gratitude toward the employees who were increasing the value-added.

As we can see, it took a lot to get the Toyota Production System going, so if someone with some superficial knowledge tries to make a half-hearted attempt to emulate it, the attempt probably will not go well, and the chances are quite high that it will end up being a failure. To make matters worse, the price of failure will be that the employees will not listen to management anymore. An area that is uncontrolled will start deteriorating, and it will take many times the amount of effort to bring it back to where it was originally.

For those of us who were taught the Toyota Production System by Taiichi Ohno, to hear of even one place where this has happened pains our hearts.

Even companies that have been doing TPS or Lean for a long time may be at risk. Even though TPS is the method that is being used in production, if it hasn't been part of the required management training, it's existence is put in danger each time there is a change in management, and it may tend to become just a set of tools. It also really saddens me when I see this.

Good kaizen creates an environment in which work is meaningful. To sustain and manage a work environment like this, it is crucial to train people in the management of a Lean organization. Please use this book to that end, and make it your mission to create a workplace where smiles are everywhere and kaizen is happening all the time.

This book is a collection of my thoughts and experiences of 40 years in trying to create that kind of wonderful workplace at Toyota Motor Corporation, Toyota Motors' Taiwan plant. I have compiled all the key points that I have learned in those years.

In Chapter 1, I have written down 15 sayings of Taiichi Ohno that I heard either directly from him or via my supervisors. I have written down what the words mean and how the Toyota Production System was deployed throughout Toyota.

In this chapter, I am hopeful that you will see the importance of the role of top management in the deployment.

In Chapter 2, I go into more detail on what exactly top management should do and how to go about doing it. Ohno really understood this role very well and acted it out. I also discuss the four stages of things, which will be very useful when visiting the gemba or the place where the action takes place.

Chapter 3 is about the role of the manager. I have written down exactly what the role of the manager at the front line should be. There are a lot of details about what the supervisor should do, but I felt that the role of the first-line management always seemed to be combined with that of the supervisor. This resulted in unclear roles and responsibilities, and I wanted to correct that.

What's also important is to understand what is needed in order to manage a Lean/Toyota Production System organization. There are a lot of motivational elements in both the production system and the management system in the Toyota method, but I see those elements being discarded. The reason for this chapter is that I wanted to underscore the importance of having a vibrant and happy workplace and to teach management how to get there.

Chapter 4 covers how one deploys the Toyota method in a foreign country that has a different culture. I am Japanese, so I wrote from a Japanese perspective. There are many things that are different between Japan and the rest of the world. A lot of our success factors can be transferred to other countries, but some things cannot be copied. Please be careful when deploying a program such as Lean or TPS.

The top management and middle management will play a very crucial role in ensuring the success of the deployment. I am hopeful that some of my detailed experiences can be useful in helping the management see itself as the main driver in creating a vibrant, continuous kaizen type of environment in the workplace.

CHAPTER 1

---◆---

LEARNING FROM MR. TAIICHI OHNO

Lesson 1: No One Really Understood What I Was Saying, So I Had to Go to the Gemba and Give Detailed Instructions

This is an excerpt taken from Taiichi Ohno's writings at the time of the commemoration of Toyota's first automotive plant (the Honsha plant) in 1988:

> In 1963, we deployed kanbans throughout the factory. There was no grand design for this, so even we didn't know what would happen. The impact of the words "increase productivity," "limit overproduction," and "use fewer people" could not really be calculated. No one really understood what I was saying, so I had no choice but to go to the gemba and give detailed instructions.

The first time Ohno's name appeared on the manager roster was in 1944, when he was a manager of the Toyota automotive arm. At that time, he was the manager of assembly;

this department spent at least the first week of each month "gathering parts," which meant that the assembly line was actually working only two weeks out of the month. In 1945, he became the leader of the machine shop, and that was the start of what the world now knows as the Toyota Production System (TPS).

Ohno spent the next 16 years in the Honsha plant establishing the many foundational elements of the TPS, such as multimachinery handling, multiprocess handling, visual management, one-piece flow, and kanban. This was not done overnight, and, as Ohno has reflected, it was done within his sphere of influence at the time, and as his influence expanded, he tried out new methods.

In 1963, Ohno finally became the factory manager of the Honsha plant, and he decided that areas such as the foundry and forging, which at the time were not connected to the machining plant and the assembly plant, would be joined to those plants by kanbans. In short, he decided that the whole plant needed to be joined together. When we look at Ohno's quote, we can see that he was determined to see this through and make it a success.

People in the forging and foundry areas were a lot tougher than the people in the machine shop had been, and so Ohno himself took the lead in cutting waste, increasing value-added, and making good-quality parts.

When we see how Ohno implemented new things, we can note the following key success factors:

1. Hands-on role modeling by top management
2. No compromises, no fear of failure, and no giving up halfway with results that were "half good"

3. Recognizing that it would take time for things to
   become sustainable and for the people working there
   to be able to improve and do kaizen, so a long-term
   follow-up had to be part of the process

Because of this, top leaders must avoid short-term changes
in policy. The reason that we have the Toyota Production
System is that Ohno stayed in production for a long time and
focused on making it work.

Getting Back to the Point

In these sections, which I have called "Getting Back to the
Point," I will be discussing experiences that I had based on
Ohno's teachings and the things he said.

I was deployed in Toyota's machine department in the
headquarters plant in 1968. I spent an hour listening to the
department head give a speech about "the mindset and heart
of the new employee," and then I was told, "Your job will be
at the Kamigo plant, so go there immediately." I basically
spent one hour at the headquarters plant and then was at the
Kamigo plant the rest of the time.

When I arrived at the Kamigo plant, there were a lot of
engineers from the headquarters plant who were there to get
a new production line up and running. The factory where the
first Mark II model was made was in the middle of a trial-
and-error process of trying to get parts to flow on automatic
lines, modifying and optimizing equipment, and deciding
how to detect and show abnormalities—all under the direct
supervision of Mr. Taiichi Ohno.

"Hey, newbie, get up on the gangway where you can see
the andon"—I remember standing up there. The engineers

were working very hard, and I could see the stress and pressure on their faces. This was because Ohno would soon be arriving.

When Ohno came, all of us went to the place where we could see the andon the best, and we went to each workstation where there had been a stoppage. An explanation of why the stoppage had occurred was given, and the maintenance staff was then called to make the necessary changes. It was right at the time of the Mark II debut, and we were having a hard time making the engine. Every day Ohno would come to the gemba and give commands. When he found areas where the handoffs and connections from one line to another were not good, we often had to spend weekends on the construction and modification tasks, sometimes even going without sleep. He would come on Monday to see what we had done. If we heard the words "I think it was better before," we would have to spend another weekend putting it back the way it had been.

For Ohno, the way of working that was being developed was going to be the foundation for all other lines, so he was very engaged in the process. He would always come to the gemba, and if he didn't like what he saw, we had to keep changing it until it was satisfactory. Even I, the new guy, could see that Ohno was also seriously thinking about the best way to do things. I thought to myself, "I now know the meaning of trial and error."

I once asked my boss, "Why don't we leave it as is, and then change it when the next project comes around?" He told me, "If we keep something that is not good, then someone will copy it. That's why we have to fix it right away." He then continued, "We mustn't notice a problem, but pretend that we don't see it and walk by. If you think of the person who has to work there and has to deal with that situation, you shouldn't be able to let it go." When I heard these words, I thought, "I have come to work with a really wonderful team."

The seriousness of top management has been transferred to the people below, and I think that's why I got this kind of answer from my boss. I wasn't part of Toyota in 1963, but I am sure that the casting and forging areas also went through a period when Ohno visited them daily and worked with the local management to build up a workplace that could perform.

Lesson 2: Kaizen Equals Getting Closer to the Final Process

This phrase was hardly used by people at Toyota, which I think is why it stuck in my mind. It seems like a simple phrase, but many people have told me that it is confusing, so I will explain the background to the situation.

When I was around 30 years old, I was working as an engineer in the headquarters machining plant. I was on the number 3 truck undercarriage line. This line was synchronized with the main assembly line and supplied parts to it. The final process was to do a quality check, and sometimes that took a long time, delaying the delivery of parts to the main line and causing a stoppage. As a result, this problem was interfering with the stability of operations.

In order to keep the main line from being adversely affected by this, we moved the parts line to a shop next door and delivered finished parts to the main line. (Basically, we disconnected the subline from the main line and delivered finished parts to the main line.) As you might expect, we had *solved the problem*, as the line stoppages to the main line had ceased. When I reported this to Mr. Ohno on the gemba, he said, "Yes, we have fewer main-line stoppages, but the time required for adjusting on the subline has not changed. Kaizen equals getting closer to the final process. Now, however, it is further away."

Our job as engineers was to find the reason for the variability in the process and change the conditions so that good product could be made in an environment that didn't require lots of effort. Because production engineering couldn't do this, we had just run away from the problem.

"If you lack skill, you can't get closer to the final process." How important it is to get the right conditions in place to make good parts. I felt that I had learned a fundamental truth about production at the time.

At the same time I thought how impressive it was that Mr. Ohno could see the real issue. I was also embarrassed. We had had no intention of running away from the problem, but the result of our actions had been to choose the easy way out, and to top it off, we thought that we had done a good job! "What are you guys doing?! Get it back to how it was before!" would have been an appropriate remark for Mr. Ohno to make, but his actual comment was more of a philosophical nature that really encouraged us to find the root cause of the variance and get the subline back to where it belonged—closer to the final process.

I think Ohno knew that our young group had done this without ill intent and felt that it was better to do something and fail than to do nothing at all. If you're up at bat and you are going to strike out, it's better to swing and miss than not to swing at all. Just by swinging the bat at the ball, you are going to gain some experience. We felt that we had learned a lot about kaizen when we struck out swinging.

When you think about it, the less inventory you have between processes, the closer you are getting to the end process. The same is true when you join processes. It was a simple sentence that had profound meaning for me. Ever since, I have asked myself and my staff to go check to see whether a change has gotten us "closer to the last process."

Getting Back to the Point

There are a lot of so-called kaizen or improvement events out there that actually go further away from the last process. For example,

- Outsourcing the rework process to a vendor
- Outsourcing a deburring process
- Outsourcing the separation of good and bad parts to a third party
- Outsourcing the removing of the runner and gate (which are not required in the final part, but are necessary for the making of the molded plastic) from a molded plastic part

These are the worst offenders, but they actually happen quite frequently. Well, why is it wrong to give a process to a third party? Some people may say, "That party can do it at a lower cost than we can, so outsourcing it is a good thing." The issue is that by keeping that process in-house, you keep the problem visible. If you see many people doing rework, it should motivate you to do something about it.

Things like burr-free casting and gateless molding come from the need to improve. If you cannot see the process, no one will think about it. The danger is that if something is difficult, it is outsourced; this then makes the company's engineering weaker and in the end reduces its competitiveness.

I once had a big surprise when I studied the supply chain for a certain part that we used. This particular part involved four processes. Two of these processes were done locally, another was done on the island of Kyushu (1,000 km /600 miles away), and the fourth was done on a different island. My goodness! How much work in process did we have? I was convinced that it was at least six months' worth. I am certain that this situation had a long history, but I think it was the culmination of Purchasing asking over the years, "I wonder who can make it more cheaply?"

By having a shorter supply chain and bringing it closer to the last process, a company can be in better control in case problems happen.

The effect of Ohno's "Get it closer to the last process," or, in other words, "getting things closer to the assembly line is a good thing," can be seen in Toyota's history, where all processes that came under Ohno's control as his responsibilities grew became closer to the last process.

The most important thing Ohno had in mind to reduce the production lead time was the concept of *flow*. When he was still the machine shop manager, "We initially focused on reducing the changeover times and reducing the batch sizes" (from Ohno's memoirs). He then continued, "We had people handle two of the same machines to increase productivity, but the batch sizes didn't change. We then changed the layout to put the machines in the process sequence and our batch sizes were significantly reduced."

This did increase productivity, but in order to prevent overproduction, a downstream pull/replenishment system was incorporated. This was the start of the kanban method, which actualized the just-in-time philosophy. Let's review Ohno's role and the history of kaizen that accompanied it.

Section Manager for the Number 3 Machine Shop

- Increased the span of the layout according to the process sequence and laid out the machines based on what parts they made.
- Decided on a five-piece batch size up to the assembly line and based the pull system on a five-piece batch size.
- Developed the "water strider picking method," so named because it looked like an insect called a water strider that was moving left and right on the water surface collecting parts. With this method, even though the different part lines are located in various locations, the water strider picks up the required set.
- The final process of each part line kept a minimum of five finished parts ready for replenishment, which reduced the finished parts inventory and which moved that process closer to the final process.

Assembly Factory Manager

- Decided on making five of the same cars as one unit and linked the assembly shop and machine shop with carts pulling a five-car set of parts at a time.
- The carts that carried the five sets of parts were treated the same as a kanban and were called "kanban carts."

Headquarters Factory Manager

- Linked the machine shop with the forging and casting plants using kanban.

Thereafter

Put the skill into the machines and, by eliminating the need for skilled artisans, went from a part-based layout to a setup in which the part making and part assembly for different cars were in the same area. This pretty much completed the evolution of getting the process closer to the final assembly.

Collecting the parts that had the same takta time (pace) in the same area allowed the teams to eliminate a lot of the waiting time associated with making parts. This also allowed for an easier way to structure the combination of work and reduced the losses associated with combining different jobs.

Other

Innovated in many other ways, such as the tsurube or well bucket method, single-minute exchange of dies, kitting, and the trolley method, to get everything closer to the last process.

I will sound like a broken record soon, but Ohno made changes only in the areas that he directly controlled. He never touched areas that were not under his control. Even if there is a highly skilled technician with a great method, going beyond the bounds of one's authority will not work. That is why the role and responsibility of top management is so important.

Lesson 3: You Need by the Line Only the Parts for the Car You Are Assembling Now

We were told that all you really need are the parts for the car that is being worked on now, and that we should deliver them one car at a time when they are needed. All the other parts should be put away in one location. The obvious meaning is to keep only what is needed right now, but the other reason for this is to free the workers from the difficult task of choosing the right part and instead have them focus on value-adding work. It allows for simplifying the job as well as being able to assure quality more easily. The reason for keeping all the parts in one location is so that one can see the entire inventory at a glance. Back then, we had to adjust the number of kanban cards every month. By keeping all the parts in one location and not all over the place, it was easy to see at a glance what inventory there was, which allowed us to minimize it more easily.

At the main assembly line in the headquarters plant, the line Ohno built didn't have the big parts by the side of the assembly line; instead, they were moved to the main line one by one on a conveyor. This was called the *trolley method*.

In the same way, the machine shop kitted one set of parts for the engine, the transmission, and the chassis in a box that we called a *pallet*. It looked a lot like the job of delivering meals in a traditional Japanese inn, so we called it the *haizen method* (*hai* means "to deliver"; *zen* in this context means "food").

The automotive assembly lines used to use the trolley method, but around the 1980s, because of the combining of picking and assembly work, the trolley disappeared. After that, when suppliers delivered parts, they delivered them to the area of the assembly line in which they would be used. The assembly workers picking the instructed parts by the line became the norm.

In 2000, Toyota Taiwan was trying to both increase first-pass yield (quality) and speed up the learning curve of its employees, and it developed a method for delivering one set of parts for the engine assembly to the Corolla assembly line. This was very successful, and Toyota headquarters took the idea, developed it more, and called it the SPS (set parts supply) system. We can probably say that Ohno's haizen system and trolley system came to completion with this.

Ohno's Teaching

If you make the work as simple as possible, you will have fewer mistakes and you won't have to say "obey obey" because people will obey the rules. Also, if it is simple, a method for having less inventory will be born.

Getting Back to the Point

The SPS system was developed to make inventory control easier, speed up learning the job, increase quality, and simplify the job—all of which were realized, but there were a lot of other nice surprises.

- *Transportation time was reduced.* The biggest initial problem was the increase in transportation time needed to deliver one kit at a time. To reduce this, we standardized the box size, which allowed us to automate the delivery system. This drastically reduced the work hours spent on delivering parts compared to the old method.
- *The length of the assembly line was shortened.* By taking away the parts from the assembly line, our line became 30 percent shorter. Up to this point, we had had a mixed model line, which was used for a long time. Even if we were making a new car, the old assembly line made work hard. We started using the method of making a new low-cost assembly line that could take advantage of all the new technologies every time we had to make a new type of automobile.
- *Availability of supervisors and engineers for problem solving was increased.* A lot of our supervisory staff's time had been taken up by the need to sort out parts and deal with assembly mistakes. With these tasks eliminated, supervisors were able to focus on the value-adding assembly tasks, as well as on attaching processes that drastically reduced our internal defects.
- *Staff could focus on developing a new line concept.* With management and supervisory staff increasing their abilities, they were able to focus their talents on making a new line, which was great for management

motivation. SPS's goal is to simplify the assembly and kanban management. Just being able to deliver one set of parts to the worker does not mean that we have arrived, however. Most assembly lines are multimodel lines, which means that different types of cars are built on the same line one after another. That means that in the current situation, the employee has to perform a mental changeover, and will have to keep concentrating so that he does not make a mistake. Also, because different cars are being made, the worker will not necessarily attach a part at the same place. If we are striving for "simple," we need to challenge ourselves to do the following:

o Make a dedicated assembly line for each car.
o Dramatically reduce the assembly line cost structure.
o For the new cars, use the latest technology on an assembly line that you build yourself.

The management can see the next stage, which allows it to chase its dreams more.

Lesson 4: Building in Batches Stunts the Growth of Your Operations (Don't Combine Kanbans and Build a Group of Them)

The final year in which Ohno drilled the machine shop was 1977. I remember that this was the longest and also the toughest period when our improvement efforts were under Ohno's direct supervision. He would come to the gemba day in and day out, and he never gave us a moment's rest. In addition, there was a lot riding on this effort, so we were told things we had never heard before. The focus was on the shop cutting the gears. Ohno saw the production kanbans on the line and started in on us:

Ohno: How come you have three of the same kanbans in a row?

Us: We are producing in lots. Once we get three kanbans, we then make the parts.

Ohno: Why don't you just make them in sequence when you get a kanban?

Us: It takes an hour to change over the gear-cutting machine.

Ohno: How long have you been doing this?

Us: For a long time, sir.

Ohno: A long time. I see. OK, from now on, you need to make the gears in the same sequence that you receive the kanbans in.

What he meant was that we had to do a one-hour change-over on the machine every time we had to make a new type of gear. Just because Ohno said, "Do this" didn't mean that our changeover time of one hour had been reduced. Furthermore, he would come over every day, so there was no way of fooling him. We were spending more time changing over the machine than we spent making parts, so we started running into part shortages on nearly all the parts. When the downstream pull transportation person showed up, he was about to put the kanbans in the "shortage" box. Ohno stopped him and had him call over the supervisor of the machine shop. "Don't put the kanbans in a box. You need to let the supervisor know. Give the kanbans to him by hand. Let him know that there is a part shortage, and you stay here until the parts are made. Going home empty-handed is meaningless, right?"

I wrote this in very gentle language, but it was a lot more combative, and one day the "shortage box" disappeared from the factory. From that day on, none of us knew what Ohno was trying to do, and Ohno wasn't clear with us. He just came, and, "You're making parts in the same sequence as when you get the kanbans, right?" was all we heard. Someone finally said that maybe Ohno was saying that we needed to reduce the changeover time on the gear-cutting machine. All of us were adamant: "No way; that can't be done." Still, if we didn't attempt it, we could not do what he was asking of us, so we got together the design engineers, production engineers, and all the other departments, explained our predicament to them, and discussed well into the night how we could have an easier changeover. After we tried out our ideas, in the end we had got the changeover down to less than 10 minutes. Actually, in the late 1970s, the stamping press machines were already doing changeovers in less than 10 minutes, and this episode was six years after that.

The gear-cutting machine was one of those processes that just had a long changeover time. Because of that, it was making parts in batches, and that method had been working out OK. This kept us from seeing the need for reducing the changeover time, which is something that I really regret. It was true that reducing the changeover time was going to be hard, but the mistake was that we had accepted the long changeover time as a fact of life.

> Building in batches stunts the growth of your operations. Don't combine kanbans and build a group of them. Produce in the same sequence you get the kanbans.

Again we had to wait until the last minute to learn something important. It just showed us that we really weren't growing as much as we ought to have been growing.

Getting Back to the Point

I suspect that there are still a lot of areas where people collect kanbans (orders). "We've figured out the pattern, and we will build batches in this logical fashion" is not what real improvement looks like.

Here are some definitions of proposed solutions:

- *Batch logic.* Collecting the kanbans (replenishment signals) until you have a group of a certain size and then making the order
- *Pattern production.* Putting the kanbans given to you in a certain sequence that makes the changeovers easy to do

These solutions may seem like a great idea from the manager's or supervisor's perspective, but it's important to remember that those who live by patterns will die by patterns. Collecting things in piles or collecting kanbans can make things easy, but anyone can do that. That is not real kaizen.

Unfortunately this idea of collecting kanbans and then starting work has become quite commonplace. Even if changeover times have been reduced, the batch sizes remain the same, so the time saved is just used for more production. I understand that we have to be competitive in the global marketplace and that each area wants to look good, but I would strongly advocate moving away from local efficiency to an overall efficiency in which stoppages are lessened and the overall flow is taking shape.

If you allow people to collect orders and work in batches, they start thinking only about what is easiest. Stick to the principle of making each order in the sequence in which you get it. Ohno told us that the minimum kanban size should be five. We kept doing kaizen until we could flow things in sets of five. That was tough, but it's something we should not forget. Production and mechanical engineering are about fighting the constraints to flow. This incident reminded me never to forget that it's a fight, and a fight isn't easy.

Lesson 5: Nine Out of Ten, One Out of Ten

Unless there is a major issue, nine out of ten managers can increase their productivity numbers when volumes are increasing. However, there are very few managers who can increase their productivity numbers when volumes are going down; even keeping the productivity numbers constant in such a situation will be difficult. Maybe there will be one out of ten people who can do that. "Well, it just means that there really aren't many people like that" is what Ohno used to say frequently.

When volumes are down, most managers will say, "When I adjusted my manpower to reflect the new volumes, even though the line was connected, there were a number of locations where we couldn't divide up the work properly. That caused some waiting, which is why I have more overtime," or something like that.

Actually, this is a problem with the layout of the line. The truth is that those problems always existed, but because their effects were minor, we just ignored them. But when the volumes went down, the problems surfaced and caused lots of waiting.

Ohno noticed this phenomenon and pushed through the concept of "productivity keeping lines even with low volume." In Japanese, we called it making *shojinka* lines. The first model line at Toyota was the transmission line used in small trucks. It has machining and assembly processes. Use the process that has waiting as the end of the line, and lay out the work so that it is in a straight line. We used to call this line "an eel's sleeping quarters" because of its straight and narrow shape, or the "one brush stroke line" because the movements of the parts could be drawn with one brush stroke (there was no need to go back or out of the area). We changed the number of parts that were being machined at one time, automated the setting of the parts, and even added auto-kick-out mechanisms on the machines to eliminate the waiting areas.

One person moved from right to left through all the processes. When she had gone through all the stations, all the necessary parts for one car had been made. What that means is that we modified the processes so that they would make only one car's worth of parts.

Our engineering staff worked on the line, too. Its job was to find out what the issues were and how things could be improved. Because of this effort, when production volumes went up or down, we were able to adjust the number of people in the line and keep the productivity in the line constant. It was our first shojinka line.

In the automotive industry, production volumes are adjusted very often. First, you develop your productivity on low-volume lines and have all the waiting time at just one area of the line. You will be a lot more effective if you develop a strategy for kaizen—are you going to focus on reducing machine breakdowns or the labor time? I will keep repeating myself, but because all the "remainder" time is in one location, no matter where you improve the line, if the saved time equals one person's worth of time, you can now take out one person from the equation. If there are many branches in the line, that means that there are many remainder points for labor time. You may have made certain processes more efficient, but this won't result in a cost reduction. The first step is to take away all the branches and make it one continuous line. It will be a lot easier to work on reducing the remainder time and getting your cost savings in terms of people if you do this.

Any improvement you can make when production volume is down will be multiplied when the volumes go up again, so use the extra time you have to work on issues that you didn't have time to look at when you were busy. The low-volume time won't last long, so work hard and get the results. This is really the test of a good manager.

When production volumes go down, it's not that we have more machine stoppages. It's just that they affect us more. Productivity going down is something that we would expect. However, if you are constantly improving the work area by doing such things as reducing machine stoppages and reducing the number of hand tools needed, you will have a great bench strength in your area. When production volumes go down, I can see which managers are really doing their job. Also, depending on how much effort you put into your work area when volumes are down, you will be rewarded accordingly when volumes go up again. To get an environment in which you get the "one in ten managers," you need to deal with the reasons why people and parts can't move.

Getting Back to the Point

I wrote before that when volumes are down, you have a chance to work on things that you normally cannot, but it really is true. It's actually a very welcome opportunity. Business success largely depends on whether top management notices the opportunity or throws it away and lets it pass by. Actually, most managers do notice and do take action, but they don't realize that the action they are taking will affect things negatively. Examples of this are letting people take time off or making the production early and shutting down for a day.

Here is what you should do: first, collect all the extra people. Then look at the flow of money. How many orders do you have out there? What are you asking your suppliers and contractors to do for you? Look through them one by one. During the period when production is going down, few things are likely to be urgent, and for those that are, there will always be a reminder from someone. Can we do something a different way? Can we make it ourselves? Is the construction we are asking for doable by the extra people we have? A company with a lot of history will have lots of opportunities like this. Once you do that, your extra people are no longer extra. They are now delivering value to the company.

Also, this is a great opportunity to make some jigs and simple equipment, and maybe even automate some processes and try to do them yourself. When you become busy, the people will go back to the line, but the experience of making something themselves will stay with them. That experience will allow them to use those short downtimes to make something that will increase the speed of improvement in your company.

In Japan, we have a saying that goes, "A disaster can turn into a blessing." I say, "A disaster can turn into growing your people."

At the very least, the factory should stop the unnecessary, nonurgent jobs that are going to outside contractors and try to do those jobs itself. That will also tell you whether the price you are paying for those services is a fair one. Making the "one in ten" managers is not just about gaining experience in kaizen, but about allowing managers to think about the risks associated with their work areas and preparing for the future. This will include making a "model line" that limits the current risk. There is a need for a bit of experience to estimate the risks that arise from internal and external factors, but at the very least, managers should be given an opportunity to think about and plan what they will do when the environment they are working in changes.

For example, there are many companies that make their goods overseas in low-cost countries and then ship them back. What they should be thinking about is, "What will we do when the labor rate goes up?" which should include making a new line or developing new equipment. "Don't worry, we'll just find another low-cost country" is not a way to grow good engineers. The companies that think of ways to make things happen even with high labor costs and that build equipment and lines to make those things happen are the ones that will keep growing.

Lesson 6: The Foreman or Leader Is the One Who "Breaks" the Standard (When You Make an Improvement and You Can Take Out One Person, Give Up Your Best Person)

In the 1940s and 1950s, when Ohno was the manager of the machine shop and was starting kaizen, there were no such positions as team lead or indirect staff members under each supervisor. Rather, each supervisor just had his direct reports.

These supervisors were called "shop daddies" (*oyaji*). They controlled people's pay and wielded a lot of authority. They were quite a force to be reckoned with, and even Ohno was not able to tell them what to do. Because of that, Ohno would work with one of the "skill men" (workers) on the line who he felt was a high-potential person.

After the improvements started taking effect and one less person was needed on the line, Ohno would take the best person—the person he had been working with—and remove him from the line. I think we can see how well Ohno was able to understand the needs of the future, his ability to develop and motivate people, and above all his ability to put a structure in place that would ensure continuous improvement.

The concept of the "outside line man" started here. Ohno used his "outside men" to increase the speed of kaizen, which also increased his staff of "outside men." After a while, Ohno designated some of these people as "team leads." (They were called Ohno leads back then.) At that time (1950–1951), Toyota didn't have any position in its HR structure called "lead." It took a few years (until 1954, to be exact) for Toyota to officially recognize the position of lead. From this time on, the outside line man was officially recognized as a person who was to do kaizen. On the one hand, the supervisor developed the standard work and taught it to the workers. He showed it, had them do it, and made sure that they did it properly. In other words, he set the standard and enforced it. The lead learned the standard taught by the supervisor, thought of better ways to do the work, and worked hard to get permission to try his new methods. In other words, he was there to break the standard.

At Toyota, the standard is there to be changed. The supervisor ensures that it is followed; the lead is there to improve it.

Getting Back to the Point

The outside men didn't stop at just being leads. Ohno took a group of them who were good at making equipment and created a maintenance department whose job was to do kaizen. These people were there to make the changes that those on the shop floor asked for. They had worked on the line before, so they understood the needs of the shop floor very well. They made simple automation devices, equipment to shorten changeover time, and machines that finished the job within takt time and allowed the worker to keep going to the next process (we call them *nagara equipment*), and a whole host of other things that greatly advanced the implementation of flow in Ohno's Toyota Production System.

Making an improvement that can take one person out results in just one person's cost being saved. If you take that person and have her make improvements, you start getting savings of two, three, four, and five people and so forth. Taking out the best person and making her improve the rest is really effective.

When a new line had to be made, those people became the supervisors, leads, and workers. They made the equipment that was to be used as well as the racks, part storage devices, and covers, and they did a lot of other work to prepare the new line for production. Once the line was up and running, many of them would stay in the line as workers.

When I joined the machining department, there were about 30 people in the group who made many useful things such as simple automation devices or a machine that could do work that was difficult to do or that required heavy lifting. The parts needed for these machines had drawings, so the workers knew what to make, but how to put all the parts together was just in their heads, so they were really fast at getting things done. I am sure that even now, many of the things the current workers are using were made by this group. During busy times, they would join the production line and help out with the extra load. This kept them from forgetting how to do the work and at the same time gave them an opportunity to find more hard-to-do tasks that they could fix when volumes dropped again. While they were working, they had their eyes open for what else needed to be fixed. This greatly helped with improving flow and improving the standard.

Lesson 7: Multiskilling Means Learning the Next Process—Keep It Flowing Until You Reach the Last Process

When Ohno came to the gemba, he would look at the one repetition of the workers' tasks. Often this would result in the creation of a "relay zone" where the worker would hand over the part he was working on to the next worker. One day when Ohno was looking, the worker doing the first process had finished his work and was in the relay zone. As it happened, the next person was not in the relay zone, so the first worker was unable to give it to her. Instead, he placed it in the area and went back to the first step of his cycle. Ohno then said to us, "The worker after this process is delayed and so wasn't there when she needed to be. If the process after you is delayed, why do you place more work into it and just leave? You haven't done proper multiskill training." He continued, "Multiskilling means that you teach the person the next process so that you don't stop the flow of work. Make sure people are helping out those who are delayed."

Up to then, all we had been taught was that you should have a relay zone so that you could hand over the baton to the next worker without losing speed. This was to buffer the normal variances we see in work. Ohno's instruction to us was to keep going until the final process, even if there was a problem downstream. If you stopped halfway, work in process would start piling up. "Don't pile up work; make it flow" and "do your best to keep the flow" were the lessons we took home.

Getting Back to the Point

Normally we are told to give the piece of work we are working on to the next person by hand in a zone much like the one in a relay race where each athlete passes the baton to the next runner to keep the flow going. In this case, Ohno said that if there was some issue preventing the next person from being in the relay zone, we should continue to work until we bumped into that person. When we had handed over the work, then we should go back to our own area and wait. This type of operation is very difficult to achieve, however.

Real multiskilling involves teaching and training the person to do all the work in the sequence of processing in his line. That way, we are preventing stoppages in the flow. The reason why we insist on transferring the piece being worked on by hand is that it clearly shows the differences between the speeds of the two workers, and the relay zone acts like a buffer to limit the damage caused by the speed variance. If we put the work pieces on a conveyor belt or if we put some racks between the workers, it becomes hard to see the differences between the speeds of the two workers. That is why we use relay zones.

This method is mainly used in machining or processing, where the work mostly involves carrying parts and placing them in the equipment, taking parts out of the equipment, and inspecting the parts; in other words, it is mostly nonprocessing work such as you would find in machining lines.

On the other hand, in assembly or fabrication, where the worker is doing most of the processing, we would not do this, since the risk of using wrong parts, missed processes, or missed parts would increase. If there was a delay, an extra person (an outside line person) would come into the line to help out, and if that wasn't enough, the line would just stop.

Going back to multiskilling in the sequence of processing: historically, when Toyota had its workers work on multiple machines of the same type, the productivity increased, but the amount of work in process didn't change much. When the company relaid out the equipment in the process sequence, however, the work in process was reduced to one. This was a huge change in the operations.

This change forced other changes, such as auto feed and auto stop of the machines, which up to now had been done manually. That freed the workers from having to babysit the machines. It also simplified the work sequence and allowed people to run many more machines.

After some time, the number of cars being made increased. The production lines then morphed into automobile type–based lines, which further reduced work in process. During this evolution, a change in our management and the multiskilling efforts for the workers took place. Up to that point, it had been OK for a worker to know how to operate one machine or make one part. Now the workers had to learn how to operate all the machines and be able to make all the parts for the car. People now understood how everything fit

LEARNING FROM MR. TAIICHI OHNO   35

together. Once they were promoted to leadership and management positions, they were able to make fast decisions and
take on leadership because of this knowledge.

Processes that had previously needed special skills became
fewer and fewer, creating a line where "everyone was welcome." This allowed us to hire from a much larger base of the
population.

Just-in-time was obviously a factor, but I also think that
multiskilling and the product-based lines are historic in that
they largely contributed to "making things in a set."

I have many opportunities to visit different companies,
and lately I have been seeing a lot of multiskill boards. The
people get a circle for each of the processes they have mastered, and at a glance you can see who has what skill. The
most important thing, however, is *flow*. I think you will get a
lot more use out of your multiskill boards if you can identify
where flow is disrupted for whatever reason and link that with
the skills training.

Just to be perfectly clear, multiskilling is an activity that
we do in order to increase flow. Keep that in mind when you
are using those boards.

Lesson 8: What's That Red Circle on the Top Right of That Graph?

We used to have a monthly meeting with Ohno with all
production departments present. In the early 1970s, the
department whose turn it was to present would show a six-
month productivity increase plan, and the goal was shown
as a red circle (see Figure 1-1). This was the conversation that

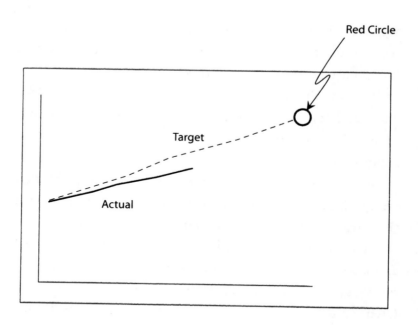

took place between Ohno and the department manager over the red circle:

Ohno: What's that red circle on your graph?
Manager: It's our goal for productivity increase this year.
Ohno: Can you do it?
Manager: We will work hard to achieve it.
Ohno: Do you know what you need to do to achieve it? Is it possible?
Manager: We will work hard and do whatever we need to do to achieve it.
Ohno: You know what's going to happen four months from now and you say you can do it?
Manager: We will do kaizen every month and work hard to achieve it.

Ohno: We don't do monthly kaizen here. Every day, every day, fix a problem or eliminate a barrier to flow. The results are what you put into it, and we are not here to do kaizen to achieve a number. If you can make a monthly plan for kaizen, why don't you just do it now?

The lesson was that achieving goals is good, but don't forget the process because you have both eyes on the numeric goal. I think Ohno was telling us not to fall into the trap of "target figures."

It's not as if you can do anything to increase productivity. If numbers are very important, we may be tempted to do whatever makes the numbers better. However, if we do that, we may be just delaying addressing the real issues. The more the managers say "targets" and "numbers," the more likely we are to get more people on the gemba becoming "number matchers." As Ohno said, productivity is just a result of our kaizen efforts. In other words, "Limit overproduction, do it with less people, and increase productivity."

If there is a department that has not met its goals, then the manager needs to go there and work with the supervisors to eliminate bad conditions and stoppages to flow. The manager's job is not to manage with numbers but to understand the reality and fix issues.

I think Ohno gave us a really wise lesson that day. It was: "Your work as managers is on the gemba. If you can't reach your targets, go to the gemba yourself and make the necessary improvements. Find the issues that are giving your people a hard time and fix them. If you can do that and work on flow, the results will come naturally." Or, to take it one step further, I think Ohno saw that target management kept managers away from the gemba and directed their attention only to numbers, and he wanted to put a stop to that.

Getting Back to the Point

I am convinced that the spirit of Ohno's way of achieving higher productivity was, "Profit is a result of focusing on flow." If you just keep focusing on the flow of materials, of course profit will follow. There are a lot of situations in which people are discussing things like "Let's change that machine to a better one and get an extra hour a day, an extra 20 hours a month" or "Let's automate that machine and reduce the manpower." These discussions take place in an office, and people are adding up hours in their heads. I feel that my biggest lesson from Ohno was not to add numbers in my head, but to go to the gemba and make the changes happen.

When you are on the gemba, you see many places where things are stagnating. Eliminating these stoppages to flow will increase our technical skill, of course get us more productivity, and make us more competitive as a company. I think many companies make their operations weaker by saying, "Just focus on making money," or, "Just give me results," with a short-term profit-minded view. When you make a profit number the target, there are many ways of achieving that. For example, maybe we can outsource the rework of a product to a cheaper company. There are many examples like this. Yes, we got the extra profit, but now we have lost the opportunity to fix this problem.

Focusing on making money is not a way to long-term success. It also doesn't make you stronger. However, we can always do kaizen. Happily, in my company we had the philosophy of the Toyota Production System. This is heavily inculcated into all employees' hearts. Making things flow and managing overproduction are what has to happen in order for the process of meeting the goals to be acceptable.

Profit comes while pursuing flow. In Japan, we have a saying, "Profit comes after good business (with the customer)." I think the same thinking permeates Ohno's Toyota Production System. In fact, I think that in Ohno's view, the "customer" is none other than the worker who is adding value. There is a very famous saying of Ohno's that is known beyond Japan. It says:

Once you do it, once you know the way, you can't help it; you have to do it. That is the kaizen spirit.

When I read this line and I look back at everything I learned from Ohno I feel him saying:

The only person adding value around here is the person on the line. Don't you feel sorry that you are making them do non-value-added work? Hurry up! Free them from meaningless tasks, get rid of things that hurt them, and make them more value-added. That is the way you live in kaizen!

Lesson 9: Are You as the Manager Having Them Do It, or Are They Just Doing It Their Way? Which Is It, Man?

Compared to the average worker or engineer on the shop floor, Ohno was a lot stricter with the shop floor management, especially the first-line managers (people who were not working on the line). Once he noticed that there were two pieces of work in process in an area where the standard work said that there should only be one. He called the manager there and said, "Why are there two pieces here? Did you tell the worker to work this way, or is she doing it by herself? Which is it?" That is where this quote came from. I was trying as hard as I could to be invisible while watching the poor manager get grilled by Ohno.

The manager was toast whichever way he answered the question, so he remained silent while getting hammered with, "Which one is it, man? Which one?"

The reason why he was being grilled was that the standard work (takt time, work sequence, and standard work in process) was decided because that way anyone would be able to do the work safely and correctly. That was clear, but if the person was not doing it according to standard, all that effort to establish a standard was useless.

The role of the supervisor is to establish the standard work, teach people how to do it, and ensure that they are doing it to standard. If the work is not being done to standard, then retraining is needed. In the same way, the manager was supposed to look at the standard work that was displayed and make sure that people were doing it that way. If not, correction was needed.

When there was an extra piece of work in process where there was supposed to be only one, it meant that the supervisor was not playing his role. If this minor infraction was let go, it would send the message to all the lines that it was OK not to keep exactly to the standard, and we would then have a workplace where standard work was not followed.

I remember that Ohno was especially strict in making sure that the shop floor standards were being followed. I feel it was because he wanted his managers to display strong leadership in making good products, safer, faster, and at a lower cost.

Getting Back to the Point

Ohno got terribly upset when standard work, which the gemba was supposed to develop and then manage, was not followed. He was extremely hard on the managers of the shop floor, as I witnessed numerous times. Quite often, when we were giving a presentation on one line and he saw something wrong on another line, he would ignore the presentation, go to the other line, and have the people there fix the problem.

Once the people had mastered the standard work, the next step was to take out a person or reduce inventory and then figure out the whole process again. Because standard work was the basis of improvement, trouble was sure to follow if the standards were just posted but not followed. When you visit the shop floor, you can immediately see how well the manager is managing her area. In fact, going to the gemba is a great way to see how good a job the manager is doing.

There was another reason why Ohno was so adamant about standard work. The standard work told us the takt time, which was the pace at which we had to make things. Different cars had different takts (paces) to which we had to make them. With everyone working to takt time, we could level out the production and the whole factory would have a sure foundation for making things smoothly and efficiently.

Lesson 10: Standard Work for the Andon Is, "Go There When It Flashes"

This was the answer Ohno gave when someone posed the question, "How should we define and show the standard work for the outside line people?" during one of the meetings with the production staff.

For people on the line who are working in a cyclical fashion, showing one cycle of work on the standard work sheet is enough, but for areas that are heavily automated or for people who are there to solve problems on the assembly line, defining their work was a lot more difficult, and hence the question. These people's main job is to go where the problem area on the line is (as shown by the andon) and fix it.

What is the standard work for things when you don't know when they will occur or where they will occur? The answer was quite simple: "Once the andon flashes, start moving; go fix the problem." By the way, we said the same thing to our maintenance staff—"Go to the gemba that calls you"—and to the transportation staff—"Be at the display board and deliver parts in the sequence in which people call you. If there are no requests, just stay there and wait."

I know many people who would be extremely uncomfortable with the idea of people just waiting—and there were many in Toyota at the time who felt that way, too. I felt that what Ohno was trying to teach us was, "Don't make things complicated."

"When it flashes, go" is actually the same instruction that the kanban has, which is, "When the kanban comes off, go and fetch some parts," or, "When the kanban comes off, make some parts." "When one kanban comes off, make it," and, "when the andon flashes, go" were both important teachings of Ohno's spirit to do things in a standard size.

Getting Back to the Point

"Don't waste your time making standards when no matter what you write, you will always be wrong, as things won't work out that way. Don't make the tools on the gemba hard to use." Keep things simple and clear, and think of how you can reduce the number of times people call you. If you do that, you will improve the flow.

In fact, the outside line person started out as a person whose main job was to make improvements. If you give these people some work to do when there are no issues for them to deal with, they will not be able to address problems when they occur. While it may look good on paper to have the team leader do actual work when there are no issues, this puts too much pressure on the system and causes dysfunction in real life.

Even as it is, there are a lot of calls for help, so if the team leader is doing actual work, she will just make more people wait. We are trying to make flow, but now our people are the biggest obstacle to it. Why did we put an andon up in the first place? The whole logic of the andon system starts to collapse.

When the andon is not flashing, the team leader's job is to find the root cause of the last andon flash and figure out a way to keep it from happening again. That's it.

Let me give you the historical background of the andon system and what the thinking behind it was. The first andon was put on the engine machining line in Toyota's Honsha plant. After more and more andons were put on lines, the company standardized the light colors. When you felt that you were going to be late, you pushed the call button, which lit up the andon yellow light. If you could not catch up during the allocated time, then the light turned red and the line stopped.

We also added andons to machining lines, which were automated. We divided up the line into sections, and when a part didn't go through a section, that andon lit up yellow. You may think that it should have been red, but we felt that this meant, "The machine is calling us for help," so we kept it yellow. After that, we differentiated between abnormal (machine breakdown) and normal (changing of cutting tools, quality checks) issues and made the normal stoppages light up white.

Based on this, the standard became the following:

Red. Red is for fire extinguishers and fire hydrants. As much as possible, don't use red, as we want to keep it special for emergencies. For us, red was used only when there was a stoppage on the final assembly line. That meant that product was not leaving the factory. *Red is the most important color. Drop whatever you are doing and go fix it.*

Yellow. This was the color that meant a "request to come over." Whether it was a machine or a worker that was calling for some help, the color was yellow. *Yellow is the color that tells you to communicate with the worker or the machine and think about how to prevent the issue from happening again.*

White. Do things properly, make an improvement to decrease the frequency with which it calls you.

I really wanted you to see how much thought went into just deciding on the colors of the andon. There are many companies using andons. It is important for things to change with the changing environment, but I wonder if the same amount of thinking is going into what the colors used should mean. Red means drop whatever you are doing and *run*; yellow means how can you make it not flash again; white means do it properly and improve it so that you don't have to do it so often (for example, reduce the wear and tear on the tool so that you don't have to change it so often).

I hope you understand the thinking behind this. The more people you have who understand this thinking, the more people you will have who are driving improvement in the company. Ohno was very interested in the andons. If the andon lit up while he was visiting a factory, Ohno wanted to know why the machine had stopped and had people find out the root cause. If he saw a machine stoppage with no andon light going off, he would wait there until the machine had been fixed. He called those instances "lying andons" because when the andon didn't light up, people thought everything was OK.

One of the worst situations in a production facility is not being able to tell whether things are standard or out of standard (normal or abnormal). When Ohno started on this journey, it was hard to tell whether the situation was under control or out of control. I think Ohno's strictness came from a strong resolve to never go back to that kind of situation ever again.

Lesson 11: Standard Work Is the Foundation of Kanban

This is an excerpt from Ohno's writings to commemorate the fiftieth anniversary of the Honsha plant in 1988:

> The supervisor must be able to correct and improve on the worker's incorrect work method. That's why I had them put up the standard work above the line. This is the root of the kanban.

Ohno is saying a number of very important things here.

The standard work can be useful to the worker if he is confused about his job, but it is more of a visual management tool than anything else. The manager will check to see whether the work is being done according to the posted standard and, if there are mistakes, to correct them. That will keep good-quality production. At first, people posted the standard work on the line and called it kanban. (*Kanban* means "sign" in Japanese.) It is a tool to keep the facility on the path toward quality, safety, and lower cost by continuing to update and "shape up" the standard work.

"Standard work is the root of the kanban": actually there is no record in either Ohno's writings or things that he said that tells us exactly what he meant by this. "When we received the Deming Prize in 1965, I thought of kanban as our catchy phrase" and "I made up the word *kanban* to make it harder for foreigners to understand what we were doing" are documented, but neither of these really tells us why standard work was the root of kanban. However, I think that the fact that Ohno wrote this on the fiftieth anniversary of the Honsha plant (10 years after his retirement) means that there is an important message there.

When Ohno built the just-in-time system using "downstream pull," he changed the label on the parts to "kanban." And he changed the original *kanban*, which was the standard work chart that was put up on the line, to the standard work *vote* (both pronounced the same way in Japanese) to show that it came from the supervisor's intention. By doing this, he eliminated the need for a ledger to manage the shop floor. Full managerial control was now at the shop floor level, and I am sure Ohno was very satisfied with that result.

When one continues to read what Ohno wrote in the same document, he ends by saying, "I feel that in the future, we need to value the system that allows people to work without mistakes even if done slowly. Also, the supervisors need to value their employees and create their own managerial structure."

Getting Back to the Point

What does "standard work charts are the root of the kanban system" really mean? I'll share my thoughts on this. When we look at Ohno's work, we see that he takes work that is normally done in a management department and moves it to the shop floor. Even today, in many companies, something like a standard work chart is drawn up by engineers who are in management positions. The andon, part shelf labeling, management, and fixed locations are all in some way moving management from the managers' office to the gemba. I think we would find more examples of this kind of thinking if we looked more.

My personal experience was one in which we moved the part making and assembly line of a unit to another company. I worked with the other company's engineers on the move plan, the training plan, the layout, the production structure, and so on, and things pretty much went according to plan.

What we changed was how we ordered parts. Instead of having orders come from an office to the supplier, we installed the kanban system with them. They just made parts to replenish their finished goods. This was good for us in that it allowed us to change the sequence farther downstream than before.

A number of days later, someone told me that Ohno came by and said, "That is good. We eliminated a controlling office."

Basically, things do not go according to plan. If they did go according to plan, you wouldn't need managers. The kanban system is based on this logic, and it allows for fine tuning based on changes to the plan. Because of this, the "management infrastructure" needs to be located on the gemba, which is where those changes happen.

"I would like to see whatever the gemba can do itself moved to the gemba, and if there are changes, they should not come via some management office, but rather be done on the gemba in a fast and effective way." I think that is what Ohno wanted to share on the fiftieth anniversary of the main plant. Here is his entire column:

Around 1963 the kanban system was spread throughout the entire factory. It didn't start with a master plan, so even we didn't know how it would develop. Concepts like "Increase productivity while preventing overproduction and do it with less people" were ideas that could not be calculated. No one was able to understand it from the explanation, so I had to go to each area and give detailed instructions.

In the Toyota Production System, when one goes to help out another department, everyone must be able to do the work the right way, and if they are making a mistake, the supervisor needs to be able to instruct and improve the work. Because of that, we put up the standard work charts above the line. This was the root of the kanban system. Lately words take on a whole new meaning by themselves and get before the real meaning of things, but the Toyota Production System actually started out quite simply.

Placing importance on creating a structure of being able to "do the job correctly, even if slowly"; having supervisors praise and recognize their workers; enabling supervisors to follow through on their managerial goals will become more and more important. I am hopeful that the many changes that will come in the Honsha plant will be met with the appropriate response by its people.

Lesson 12: When the Worker Pushes the Start Button, He Has Stopped Moving. Can't You Guys Figure Out a Way for Him to Push Start While Still Moving?

When I was in the house (the office for the production staff), the manager in charge of kaizen received a phone call from the shop floor saying, "Ohno wants you to come." Our thoughts were, "Oh, no; did we do something wrong again?" as we ran to the place where Ohno was. He was looking at the transmission machining line, and when we got there, he said, "Look at the movement of the worker. He is stopped when he pushes the start switch." We were not too sure how to respond, as that was such an obvious thing and we had no idea where he was going with this thought. Ohno then said, "He attaches the part to the machine, walks a bit, stops, and then starts the machine. Can't you guys figure a way out where once he starts walking, he doesn't have to keep stopping to start the machine?" He continued, "Hmmmm, elevator buttons work when you just lightly touch them. I guess you have to stop if you have to push the button on the machine that hard, huh-uh-huh?"—meaning that the worker had to stop because he had to use a lot of force to push the start button.

Ohno knew that we had been using this same switch for the last few decades. The maintenance manager and I had both been preparing ourselves for a tongue-lashing, and we were relieved to find that he was only talking about switches. Those on the kaizen staff are always making things for the shop floor, and during busy times they go and work in the line. We were told to put this experience to full use and make something that is easy to use.

In the end, we didn't use the touch switch on elevators that Ohno was talking about, but instead used a limit switch. In the past, we had developed a cam to stop the switches from breaking, so we put this experience to use and in two days had a model to show Ohno. He saw it and gave us the OK.

When we actually used this, the worker tired a lot less and the walking time went down by around 10 percent, which was a big surprise for us. After this, this limit start switch concept was used throughout Japan.

Maybe Ohno was thinking, "Elevator switch—touch only—we can use that somewhere—oh, yes, start switches," which I think is why he said, "Can't you guys figure out something huh-uh-huh?" Whenever Ohno thought of something, he said, "Come to the gemba," and he used his own pool of people to squeeze their brains until they had a good idea of how to make things flow. Parts were flowing and workers were flowing. I think he kept the ideal in his mind all the time, which is why he was able to give these kinds of directives.

Getting Back to the Point

There was a kaizen group in each production department. They were made up of people who had a special talent for making things, and their job was to make things that the shop floor requested that would make the job easier. They really got excited when the request was for something that had never existed anywhere else. There was a difference in the talent level in different departments, but that difference created a healthy competition, and every year these groups would bring new contraptions into the world. We had high expectations of the kaizen group, and it always seemed to deliver beyond our expectations.

In the organizational structure, the group was between the direct and indirect departments, so during peak times it just maintained a skeleton crew and the rest of its members helped out with production. We encouraged them during those times, telling them that it was training to find more useful things they could make for the people. We also took particular care that they weren't kept too long in production so that their equipment-building skills didn't decrease.

We felt really bad that until Ohno told us, "The worker has to stop to push the button," we hadn't noticed anything wrong. Because of that experience, however, we were determined to make improvements before Ohno could say to us, "Hey, this is a similar situation—fix it!" One day we noticed a worker holding the impact wrench in place, and so we made a switch that allowed him to walk away once he had set the tool on the nut.

Automation in which something is set manually is called "one-touch automation." It is much cheaper than full automation, and it can be done a lot more simply as well. Because of Ohno's setting us on fire, we were able to see a lot more opportunities for this one-touch automation and were able to make many similar improvements.

Lesson 13: You Bought an Expensive Machine, and Now You Want an Expensive Foreman or Engineer to Run It? Are You Mad?

It was at the chassis factory and we had just installed our first transfer machine. It was an expensive and important machine, so to learn how to use it quickly, we had put our best supervisor on it. We thought that by doing that, we could get to a safe and stable production level quickly. I suspect most companies would do the same thing.

However, when Ohno came around to see how things were going, he saw the leader working very hard. That scene told him, "We are working very hard, and I am the only one who can use it," and we heard the words that are the title of this lesson.

The people who were working on the installation—the production managers and the engineers—were all at a loss as to why he would say such a thing and didn't know what to do. At that time, one of the manufacturing engineers, who was kind of like an interpreter for Ohno and had taken a lot of concrete actions based on Ohno's verbiage, understood what Ohno meant and explained it.

> We started out with a machine-based layout; at that time you needed a special machinist to operate each machine. Then we added intelligence to the machines, separating the manual and the machine work so that you didn't have to be a specialist to run the machine. Now, you've spent even more money and you've put your best person on the machine! Besides, if we look at what this supervisor is doing, he is just trying to restart the machine when he runs into a problem instead of solving the root cause. Right now, if he takes a day off, production will stop. Let's clarify the problems and fix them so that anyone can run this machine.

By convincing everyone that this was what we had to do, and by setting the standard at where a worker on the line could run the machine, we were able to clarify the issues and fix them one by one. The supervisor was now able to be offline again and able to support the direct people.

When we first purchased the transfer machine, it was labeled as a "one-person-control machine," meaning that one person was needed to operate it. Because of this experience, the standard was changed, and the next transfer machines we purchased were all no-person-control machines.

Getting Back to the Point

I think most people understand the kind of thinking mentioned before, but all of us are worried about whether things will go well once we put this thinking into practice—even more so when we have some production equipment that has a deadline to be met. I think Ohno was thinking the following:

> I know they are just throwing a supervisor in there and making it his problem. That's not doing us any good for the future. This is a great opportunity for me to show them what kind of mindset we need to have.

This is why he said what he did to us. When I heard this story, I remembered another one of Ohno's hard teachings. It was:

> When you make an improvement and you can take one person out, you must take out the best person from the line.

There are three good reasons to do this.

- The person will now be able to look at her work from a different perspective, which will make it easier for her to fix it. Quite often, a good employee is subconsciously compensating for problems, so she doesn't even know that those issues exist.
- You get the most powerful force from the line and focus it on improvement.

- The people who are left are motivated to be taken out of the line, so it helps to create a positive attitude as well as seeing change as a reward.

This is what we had been doing, but then suddenly our thinking changed when we bought a new machine. It is really important to keep repeating the principles and thinking to the people who work there; otherwise, they will be forgotten. I think there are many people who are very thankful for the people who came before them for creating the kind of work atmosphere they now enjoy.

Lesson 14: Engineers in Production Become the Horizontal Threads in the Cloth

In 1960, Ohno brought together the engineers who were assigned to the production department and gave them the following lesson:

The important departments required to make a car, such as design (function and quality of the car), procurement, and production engineering (equipment function, procurement price, duration) are like the vertical threads in a cloth. Yes, we can build a car with just these vertical threads, but no matter how well we organize these departments, with each one working toward its own goal and toward what is best for it, things will not work out, and we will not have a good production system. As a result, we will be making things in a sea of muda. The processes to make a car are very long and hard to see. There is muda happening everywhere to such an extent that no one can really measure it.

You engineers in production need to look at the entire process flow and look for the overall efficiency. That is the important job given to you. More specifically, look at the four elements (processing, inspection, transportation, and waiting) that directly affect quality, safety, cost, and delivery. Grab the vertical threads strongly and push them to work together to make good products at a lower cost and faster. That will make us a strong cloth. Then take the results of your work and give them as feedback to the vertical departments so that they can learn from it and use those lessons in their next project.

With this talk, Ohno showed the engineers what was the ideal state of production. It was that the gemba (where things were being made) took leadership and, without fear of failure, through trial and error made a better working environment. He also forcefully pushed this point with the engineers in production. Because Ohno took his machinists, made them the horizontal threads, and was able to get significant results, the whole company took notice, and in 1958 all five production departments and the related production engineering and inspection departments got a horizontal thread group added to them.

Engineers in production become the horizontal threads in the cloth—I think this is a great saying, and it still holds a lot of significance even today.

Getting Back to the Point

Right now, we think that things like layout by process sequence, low manual labor content equipment, downstream pull, and set load transport are just logical and make sense. But all these concepts were the result of a lot of working through a lot of difficulties and hardships. To bring that point home, I want to share, using a couple of examples, just how un-just-in-time and how un-jidoka-like Toyota was between 1945 and 1965.

Back then, people got monthly production schedules, and in order to be efficient in their own processes (there is quite a big difference in the definition of efficiency nowadays), they would do the following:

- Try to have the smallest number of changeovers—big batch production.
- Avoid problems caused by parts shortages by having lots of inventory and overproduction waste.

FIFO was impossible with this kind of thinking; no one knew what kind of analysis to do when quality issues were found, and the labor hours required to "get back to normal" were very expensive.

On top of that, people's pay was determined by how much their team produced, so the more production they did, the more the employees made—an obvious incentive to overproduce. Of course the fewer the number of changeovers required, the more they could produce. I am sure that in such an environment, the concept of making only what was needed today, then changing over to another product fell on deaf ears.

The overproduced parts weren't even put on shelves in an orderly way so that one could access them easily, so just trying to find the right parts was extremely painful. Today, the parts marshaling areas (Toyota does not use the term *warehouse*) are not there to collect parts; they are areas designed to ensure the transportation of the "correct parts in the correct volume at the correct time." Back then, however, the marshaling areas looked like anything but this. They were not organized, and things were shoved into any small space that opened up. Because of that, a great deal of time was spent searching for, finding, and trying to gain access to the parts. Ohno started out by putting parts in order on three-level shelves.

It was in this kind of environment that Ohno forcefully pushed through the concept of flow. By incorporating jidoka into the equipment, laying it out in process sequence, and moving processes that were traditionally outside the normal flow, such as plating, heat treating, and painting, into the overall flow, he eliminated transportation and work in process and eliminated the concept of teams of people who did only one process. In such ways, he kept removing barriers to flow. These were all stories I heard from the people in the machine shop.

After this, the concept of flow kept advancing. Parts that required the same kind of skill to make were brought together to be managed by one team. Afterward, a water-strider (*mizusumashi*) was used to join the assembly line and the parts-making line by pulling one set of parts at a time. In another upgrade, the parts required for a certain model of automobile flowed continuously into the main assembly line. This then became the foundation of the modern unit line.

As the concept of flow started incorporating a wider area, the area to be managed also increased. The Japanese concept of "promote from within," which everyone believed in, helped people use their talents and experience, which in turn produced good business results. This is why we often say, "Making things means making people."

From here on, jobs will get more specialized and individuals will be held more accountable, which I am sure will lead to a lot more silo mentalities (in Japan we call this sectionalism). In a factory, the work done upstream all flows down to the factory. If one looks upstream, he can see how those departments are thinking. If people aren't working as a team or cooperating, that will at least cause problems at the gemba level. The job of the engineer will become even more difficult, but it's at these times especially that we need those horizontal threads to go between the vertical threads so that at the gemba, all aspects of production feel that they are pointing the same way.

Ohno put a great deal of emphasis on wording. In this book, I have used words like *horizontal thread* and *vertical thread*, but Ohno would use the technical terms. He would write out the characters (spell out the word) for people and explain them. Ohno was from Toyoda Loomworks, so he had a keen understanding of how to make cloth, but he was still a man who placed a high importance on words. He had people think about the wording, and he repeated those words often.

Let's take a look at these words again: "Engineers in production become horizontal threads." Why production? Well, all the departments and sections of the company come in as vertical threads in the production gemba.

Lesson 15: The Lowest Kanban Quantity Should Be Five

This was the answer given to a person who asked, "Is one the lowest kanban quantity?"

> Sure, you could pull one, but why would you want to do such a useless thing?

When sharing Ohno's thoughts, I must mention that the kanban quantity had to be at least five, or else risk Ohno's ire. He was "Five lot Ohno." I kept wondering how to talk about this concept. I wrote and rewrote the section, then postponed it to the final lesson in this chapter, and now I must deal with it. If I didn't include this, I could not claim to have written a book about Ohno's thinking, so I will just write down the facts and the words that I heard from Ohno directly. It will be up to the reader to try to get some meaning out of it. I hope it proves useful.

Ohno was quite adamant about the five-piece kanban. Five was the smallest lot size, and parts were kept in sections five at a time. When Ohno was in charge of the assembly plant, the welding plant, and the machining plant of the Honsha factory, the engines, frames, and transmissions were made in sets of five and the same car was made five in a row. After he became the head of the whole factory, he had the casting and forging departments think in terms of multiples of five as well and put in the kanban system to reflect that. That joined the raw materials to finished automobiles in this daisy chain of five units at a time. Ohno determined that this structure was the most efficient for the Honsha plant, and the machines had a changeover every five parts so that they could keep up with the kanban instructions. The saying was, "Get your change-overs down so that you can do one every five parts," which was the goal for all equipment.

During one of Ohno's training sessions where all the managers were present, I remember very clearly when one of them asked Ohno what the minimal kanban size ought to be. Ohno responded by saying, "I don't think we would do a useless thing like picking one or two. You need at least five, which is why I determined that five is the minimal size."

Just to add some more explanation to this, what it means is that if one took a part that had a kanban for one part on it, that was a useless thing. In fact, if there was a kanban that said, "Make one more," there would be no real need for a kanban. As an aside, in the Honsha plant, we leveled out our production in multiples of five. Sometimes we would make 10 cars of the same type if a lot of them were being sold.

Digression

The five-piece kanban that Ohno put all his effort into making slowly spread until all parts of the factory, including part machining, forging, and casting, were finally connected by multiples of five. After assembly (in terms of information flow), everything was on the pull system, so that if one knew when the assembly plant would finish work, correct decisions could be made at the shop floor level as to how much more should be made and when to stop work. This was a very efficient factory management method, and at the time only the Honsha plant was putting kanban-pulled parts into the main assembly line.

At the same time, this five-piece kanban was a way to make production more efficient. The customer was ordering in multiples of one, so making another four (which we did not have orders for yet) seemed like overproduction, which was what Ohno hated the most. For many people, this seemed like a logical conflict.

If one goes to a Toyota plant today, each car that the plant is making is different, meaning that it is making cars in lot sizes of one. The ability and techniques to make one car at a time were developed after the age of the batch of five. Even at the time, if we had made the effort to get to a batch of one, I think we could have done it, but Ohno was absolute in his opposition to that idea. Ohno was not someone who would use lack of space or lack of equipment as a reason not to do something, so obviously he had a good reason for this. Let's use our why-why analysis to see if we can understand what he was thinking.

Ohno used to say, "The profitable production is a forecasted production." If we think this way, then the pull system or the replenishment system was a "forecast"; we don't know when the part will be used next, but we will make it so that it is available. The kanban served as a governor on how far ahead we could forecast. The "forecast" that Ohno talked about was not a slippery slope or an open-ended thing, but something that had strict limitations placed on it by the kanban size.

The four extra cars made on the assembly line were also cars that had not yet been sold. They were cars that our sales department had to sell. I think this method dovetailed into the obvious function of sales, which is to "sell what is as yet unsold." In this method, the one car sold became five cars sold and became "the profitable forecast production." The four extra cars stopped becoming overproduction but turned into four profit-generating cars.

There was also no worry that these five cars would become long-term obsolete stock, as the only time we would make more would be when those five cars had been sold and we got the next order. Inventory was not growing on its own but was controlled. It's a really well-thought-out system. This method was used for quite a long while, and the salespeople played their role and ended up selling the extra cars in a manner similar to what I described.

We no longer have a car assembly line in the Honsha plant, so this issue is now one of the past, but I think it is unwise for us to write off the logic of making five at a time too easily. Doing five at a time is easy to remember and makes it harder to make mistakes; when you have too much workload, your team leader helps out. It's a very simple system.

The five at a time method accommodates both making the one for the customer and efficiency in production. It takes a complicated assembly process and makes it simple, self-contained, and clear. Methods like these are hard to come by, and I look forward to the next generation coming up with a new way to accomplish this.

---◆---

CHAPTER 2

THE ROLE OF THE TOP

The focus of this chapter is on the management needed to sustain a successful Toyota Production System implementation. It covers techniques and engineering that "wow" people and the management needed to deliver that wow.

"Profit comes while pursuing flow."

The Management and Structure Needed to Have a Successful Toyota Production System Deployment

In this chapter, I want to introduce the kind of management that is required if everyone from the top management to the lowest employee is to understand Ohno's teachings and put them into practice, and also to focus his efforts and joyfully improve his workplace.

In most instances, when a company decides to implement the Toyota/Lean system, it hires professionals in these methodologies. The majority of the training is done by "Lean experts," outside consultants who focus on the methodologies or "how to" and make a production system to go along with them. In such a situation, what often happens is that the supervisors have to learn by trial and error how to manage the new workplace. Since everything is new, trying to determine and do what is required of them takes all their efforts, and they don't have enough time left to manage the operations. The very task they were hired for—to be a steward of operations—disappears.

For a successful Lean (TPS) effort, the corporate culture as well as the management style will need to change. It's in everyone's best interests to teach managers how to manage a Lean workplace so that they can keep improvements happening and so that doing Lean becomes part of their job.

I've seen a lot of workplaces and met a lot of business managers who were very happy with the initial results of the Lean deployment, but when they tried to deploy Lean principles to other lines, not only were the results not as good, but the motivation of their employees was going down. Thus, instead of its being a great thing, Lean was adding to their stress.

I once was shown a line that had been "kaizened" in the past—I still remember it quite clearly. It was obviously a production line that a lot of people had spent a great deal of effort on creating and improving. When I saw it, however, its old grandeur was gone; work in progress was piled up in certain areas, and the company was doing only one changeover a day. It really hurt me to see something that people had put so much effort into looking so unkempt. How had it gotten to this point? I felt that I had to find the answer using the Five Whys and get to the root cause. This incident really made me think seriously about how to avoid such situations in the future.

Luckily, I was in a department at the time that allowed me to see many companies that were implementing the Toyota method. Some were doing well and were on a trajectory to keep improving. Others were just giving the method lip service. I was able to analyze these situations from various points of view, such as implementation methodology and acceptance of the system. As a result of my analysis, I came to understand that the Toyota Production System does not work very well with the traditional management style of getting orders from people in higher positions and dealing with their various demands.

Companies that start doing Lean and make various improvements to get flow going, come to require a Lean management style. In other words, as things start improving, the time will come when the rules and regulations that used to govern the company don't fit with it any more. If one understands this, corrective action can be taken, and the company can go from a traditional management style to a Lean one when the time comes. This is very important, so I will go into more detail.

I named this "Management *for* the Toyota Production System," and I put it in a booklet. We tested the theory by giving this booklet to people who had just become managers and teaching them the principles in it. However, the new managers who were the "students" had already been influenced by Ohno, so I didn't see a marked difference in how they acted.

I then became the manager of the forming department. These people were working in batches, not in the one-piece-flow or kanban method seen in the machine shop or the assembly shop, so they could understand the differences quite well. We kept the role of the leader in mind and helped people see how their role changed as we put in the new management to accommodate our new system. That helped each line improve consistently and continuously.

I also learned a lot from the forming department, which I added to my management booklet. When I became the president of Toyota's Taiwan plant (Kuozui Motors), we implemented the program not just in the factory, but also at the suppliers. As a group, we kept the focus on *flow*.

In order to have a successful flow, the skill level of production and production engineering is key. Our team included the top management from our suppliers, so each supplier also saw great benefits. It really underscored for us that if the top management is pulling the system through, much better results can be expected.

Even in production, there are times when decisions must be made by top management. For those times, it is really useful to have a sturdy information pipeline for communicating between the shop floor and top management. If you don't, you miss the opportunities to make timing decisions that will give the greatest benefit. That is why, as top management, you need to know what is going on in the gemba.

The role of top management is crucial. In companies where everyone can see that top management strongly desires results, there is a tendency to have high-pressure management (I call it management by terror). Normally this does get results, but then they tend to taper off.

Any company will improve at first. The important thing is to have a structure that allows it to continue to improve all the time. In order to create this, it is necessary not just to push on productivity, but to have a situation where the people who are doing the work understand and accept the system, are able to use their talents in their job, and are acknowledged. As I keep repeating, "Profit comes after flow." First develop people, then continue to develop people, and keep developing people all the time.

In Chapter 2, I will be mainly focusing on the foundations required for management for the Toyota Production System. The wrong definitions will often lead to the wrong conclusions, so I want to define some terms. Let's start with the word *structure*.

Companies have functions that allow the different departments to do what they are supposed to do. To enable the different functions to understand each other and carry out operations smoothly, there are rules. And operations is required to put it all together. Functions and rules are decisions, but operations is always done by people. Structure is built upon functions, rules, and operations. Normally, what people mean when they speak of structure is actually functions. Management is done by operations, and that role is given to people with different backgrounds and experience levels. No matter what, management will be largely influenced by the manager's experience, attributes, and personality. However, if people understand their function and the rules of their position along with the manufacturing fundamentals, although there may be differences, I feel that a fairly level operation is possible.

Therefore, to ensure that different managers don't result in substantially different management, I would like to introduce both the fundamentals and the methods that Toyota uses to get continuous improvement. This is the management required to operate the Toyota Production System that I learned as a worker, manager, and executive, and making it happen is the job of top management.

The Role of Top Management: People Who Can Change the Structure (Rules, Organization, and Operations) Based on Changes the Production Environment Faces

The definition of "top management" or "the head" is a person who can change the company's rules, function, and operations based on its changing needs. So when the word *top* is used, it doesn't necessarily mean the president. Ohno was the top even when he was a section manager in the machine shop.

When you realize that it took Ohno 30 years as the top to build the Toyota Production System, it really isn't a stretch to say that "for better or for worse, the success is based on the top management." However, it's quite common to hear the factory manager or head of site say to a production manager, "Well, it looks like we're going to do Lean now, so I'm going to let you drive it. I'll stop by two or three times a month to see how you're doing, OK?" The people may feel, "We'd better be serious about this, since the head of site is watching us," but this method of deployment isn't something that will last long. In fact, it's probably better not to start at all.

Things may go well at first, but then for some reason they start to not go so well, and in the end many companies will testify that they are now worse off than they had been before. Many may be puzzled about why this happens, but once standard work is in place, the flow of materials is a lot faster than it used to be, and problems that had previously been hidden start becoming very visible. There is much less work in process, so those who are repairing machines or equipment or dealing with quality assurance are no longer able to keep up with the speed required.

For companies that have a long history of doing things, attempting to put in a system that will require a different way of thinking will probably require changes in the company's structure. When a company starts moving the Lean efforts forward without knowing this, the older and more experienced workers start resisting because they can no longer do things the way they have done them before. The longer the history, the stronger the culture that allowed people to get work done under the previous circumstances, which makes it harder for them to implement a Lean culture.

A company culture is made up of its long-established rules, organization, and operations. Changing these aspects of a culture is a huge challenge, and therefore the new way will keep running into problems with "the way we do things around here." A smart set of executives will ask the question: What current rules do we have that will get in the way of our going toward more flow or more of replenishment pull style? Which of these rules will need to be changed, and how will we change them? Most likely, not only rules but the organization structure will have to change.

The solution to this is not for top management to come to the gemba and work with the workers in doing kaizen.

Its role is to understand the interrelationship between the rules, organization structure, and operations and change them step by step. Top management must be a step ahead so that the employees don't feel afraid or lost in the midst of the changes. That is the role of the top.

In the initial stages, think of your measures not as growing profit but more as growing people. Ohno changed Toyota's whole company organization by taking the time needed and by working with the people under his direct control. That helped him overcome the deeply set culture that had developed in the shop floor over the years.

The Foundation of Operations: How the Top Should Look at Things from Four Perspectives

We have examined the importance of the role of the top. If you are thinking about using the Toyota Production System in your company, you need to understand what it means to implement the Toyota Production System and what it means to develop a structure for making things. I want to explain this from a management perspective, one that is simple and easy to understand.

This is very simple, but many people seem to need a lot of time to understand it. Once you understand it, though, the rest of the "putting in the structure" topics will make a lot more sense. After you read this chapter, I would encourage you to reread Ohno's teachings in Chapter 1. I am sure that things in that chapter that were a bit confusing when you read them before will be a lot more understandable. You will probably have a clearer picture in your mind of Ohno giving directions to the people of that day.

What is important for me is that the perspective is easy to understand and that this method is actually useful for people at the top who have to manage the business, not just the production. "Easy to understand" is a very important concept in the Toyota Production System, since team leaders and supervisors have to make decisions without delay. It's important that we do not use difficult words or concepts and that we value simplicity. I have also written this section for top managers who don't understand the shop floor, but still feel that if the company doesn't change, it will lose its competitiveness or even not survive. It will be a great way for you to see problems and areas that need fixing.

As explained before, the only person who can really change the rules, the organization structure, and operations to make a company a vibrant place is the top. So in order to create an environment in which the employees and managers can use their strengths and talents, you must first learn how to view a manufacturing facility and understand just-in-time. Once you can understand the gemba and see improvement opportunities, good management that influences the whole facility and then the numbers that prove the good management will become familiar.

The Four Categories of Things

In the Toyota Production System, material flow is the most important element. Generally speaking, we call raw materials, work in process, and finished goods "things," but we can divide them into four different categories based on a value-added analysis. This is a foundational way of looking at the gemba, and if you can learn to see things this way, more issues will be apparent.

The four categories of things are the following:

1. *Waiting.* This means that nothing is being done to them. For example:
   - Parts made by an area that is working multiple shifts that are delivered to a section that is working a single shift
   - Parts made to accommodate people who are taking vacation
   - Parts needing rework
   - Maintenance parts
   - Extra parts made for the customer working more days
   - Parts needed to accommodate changeovers
   - Safety stock for equipment breakdowns or sudden absenteeism
   - Parts for design changes and plant shutdowns
   - Parts between processes on fully automated equipment
   - Finished goods waiting to be transported
2. *Being inspected.* This is the stage where judgments are being made concerning whether the things made meet the specifications and requirements. For example:
   - Work in process that is being inspected
   - Parts being carried into the inspection room to be checked

3. *Being transported.* Parts that are in the process of being transported. For example:
   • Things that are on a conveyor (before and after processing)
   • Parts that are being pulled for the next process and being carried between lines or processes
4. *Being processed.* The shape or structure of things is being changed. For example:
   • Things that are being cut by equipment or being welded or assembled
   • Things that are undergoing any structural change, such as heat treating
   • Cooling and/or quenching of high-temperature parts

All four of these categories are necessary in order for things to be completed, but when they are looked at from a work perspective, the processing category is different. Work means that the process is moving forward; in other words, it is getting closer to the final process. In the processing stage, the shape of the object changes. Shape in this case is not only the outward appearance but can also mean the hardness or structure of the object. Value is added because the shape is being changed. On the other hand, waiting, inspection, and transportation don't change the shape of the product, so no value is added. Not only that, but the time spent on those activities increases the cost of the final product.

Processing increases value.
Waiting, inspection, and transportation increase cost.

I think this makes it logical that through activities designed to decrease waiting, inspection, and transportation, labor and managerial costs decrease and the objects get closer to their finished stage. The important thing is to improve the quality of the processing and to decrease waiting, inspection, and transportation, which will increase the ratio of processing to the total time spent.

As kaizen is done, we start seeing the limiting factors based on either skill or technical ability. When these get fixed through improvement, we get a safer, higher-quality, lower-cost structure and a well-timed organization. This organization has low in-process inventory with good engineering and a highly skilled workforce.

The reduction in waiting, inspection, and transportation and the increase in the ratio of processing to the total time spent is what we call *flow*. This flow is the key to the Toyota Production System and the most important goal for the activities on the gemba.

As an example, the kanban system is just a method for trying to achieve just-in-time. Just-in-time involves delivering to the customer (the next process) what is needed when it is needed and making only the amount needed. The kanban system just uses the kanban to show the previous process what is needed, the timing, and how much is needed.

Once you increase flow, the kanban system starts fitting really well. So the first step is to join the processes together in sequence, making it a one-piece-flow line, and then put in the kanban system.

What I would like you leaders to do is to go see for yourselves the four elements in your area. At the actual place, compare how much processing is happening with the other three elements. I think you will agree with me that you have lots of opportunity for decreasing cost, which is actually encouraging.

When you do go to the gemba, however, try not to ask the people who are working there many questions. The best thing for you to do is to just keep quiet and walk around. If you start giving orders, then you may confuse people. The first step is just to understand what is going on, and that's it. If you continue to try to understand, you will see things that you didn't see before. I am sure there will be issues that you will want to raise right away, but try to control those urges. If you don't feel useful, try to think about how you will deploy this thinking and action companywide. That will be a much better use of your time.

How to Eliminate Waiting, Inspection, and Transportation

Next, we will discuss methods of reducing waiting, inspection, and transportation. Knowing this will help you have a much more fruitful time when you walk around the shop floor trying to analyze the current situation. Here are some specific actions that can be taken.

Waiting

- Write down the reason, how long the part will sit there, and the manager responsible.
- Reduce finished goods inventory; do a pull system based on a kanban.
- Reduce changeover times.

Inspection

- Try doing inspection within the process.
- Make dedicated inspection jigs for each process or each part.

Transportation

- Move processes closer together.
- Transport a fixed amount each time.
- Pull a set amount by kanban.

I am sure that if you compare the ratio of what is being processed (worked on) to the three elements of waiting, inspection, and transportation, you'll be quite surprised at how small the ratio of processing to the others really is. If the processing time for one part is one minute and it is in a box of 20, then it will take at least 20 minutes for that part to get to the next process. If you can join the processes and create a one-piece flow, you now do not need the boxes that used to hold the 20 parts, and 19 units of work-in-process inventory have now been eliminated, removing the need to use that much cash to carry inventory. It depends on the industry, but normally the ratio of processing to the other three elements is 1:100 or even 1:1,000.

Once I was visiting a factory that was making aluminum parts. The production engineer was proudly explaining improvements that had been made in the core technology of casting. After the explanation, he asked me, "Do you have any comments or notice anything?" .

I said, "The aluminum parts get heated up, processed, and washed and basically become light-emitting objects. Those objects were on pallets all over the factory, and they were so shiny that I was getting blinded, so I couldn't see anything. I was just trying to be safe and not trip over myself."

I was being sarcastic, but what I was really trying to say was, "Where's the improvement that came from your great engineering?" Not only did cash become "things," but normally those things will get more of the three elements that we don't like done to them.

The methodology of reducing the three elements is important, but for people at the top, it's more important that you think this way. Understand the scariness of inventory and try to manage with that fear in your heart.

---◆---

CHAPTER 3

THE ROLE OF MANAGEMENT: ENABLE YOUR EMPLOYEES TO DO THE WORK WELL

In order to delegate and give authority, develop people who can be delegated to and be given authority.

To All You Managers Out There

When I ask Japanese managers at various companies, "What is your role?" most of them will say, "To harness the efforts of all employees to reach the goals of the department, and to improve the safety, quality, timing, and cost of the area given to me," or something similar.

This may be something that is unique to Japan. Most people who work at Western companies have job descriptions, so when you ask them what their role is, they will respond with their job description. It will be hard to find a group of managers who will all respond the same way the Japanese managers do.

In a typical Japanese company, each department will direct more effort toward the areas that are not meeting their monthly improvement goals, and everyone will work to reach the goals in all the categories. Every company is competing, so rather than focusing on the process of kaizen or what was done, the results become the most important thing. I think that is why most Japanese managers—from those higher up to the supervisors—will respond the same way.

The interesting thing is that even though we are all governed by objectives and goals, if a problem occurs, Japanese managers will have no issues with going beyond their bounds of responsibility to help out and deal with the problem. People may think that the spirit of helping one another, having strong teamwork, and caring for one another are all relics of the past and are not found anymore. This spirit may have declined, but in most Japanese companies, it is still very much the norm and is fostered. So the fact that "my role" is not clear actually helps these firms achieve their targets.

When I was at Toyota, we all had to go through managerial training. Most of this training, however, was very general. In theory, it could be used everywhere, but if memory serves me right, that generality didn't really match the needs of each individual work area, and so the usefulness of the training was rather limited.

A manager in Toyota's production area is working in the environment of the Toyota Production System, without extra inventory and in a very fast flow. If a problem arises, within moments he may shut down his department, other departments, and even the entire assembly factory. That kind of environment requires a fast resolution, and so one has to know who to call for what issue beforehand.

Most of the managers believed that they should go to the gemba to see whether the inventory in process and between processes was correct, and whether people were working to the standard method. They also believed that they needed to invest time in eliminating areas where defects could happen.

When a problem that would seriously affect multiple departments arose, the affected departments would be notified, and they would work together on a temporary stopgap. The estimated effect and when the fix would be completed would be reported to the managers. During this time, the managers would also be working with the team to limit the damage that the problem would cause.

Managers and supervisors were always dealing with risk, so without knowing it, they were playing their role as managers in a Toyota Production System environment or in a flowing workplace. The principles were being developed in the production system, and the company culture was being created. A structure that allows people to see and feel that they are successful and are working in a line that is connected to many parts is key to developing good supervisors and managers.

I think we can see how important the structure or logic of the production system is. In a line like this, managers who can make improvements, do good risk management, ensure fast recovery after failures, and create a vibrant workplace are developed.

I feel that we need to have a general definition of a manager who can work in the Toyota Production System environment. Here are the three different management roles that I find especially important. These roles ensure that managers are looking at things from a different perspective that leads to more effective solving of issues.

Managers Are There to Create an Environment in Which Increases in Flow Happen

In most Japanese companies, the word *manager* is understood to refer to:

1. Assigning jobs and tasks to people
2. Checking those jobs and tasks
3. Having the person redo them if they weren't done right

Basically, the manager has the people under her bring her work that has been completed, checks it in different ways, and sometimes stops the job if necessary. I think many people believe that this kind of "checking" function is the manager's main job. Many managers also feel this way and are motivated to work long hours as checkers and verifiers.

I think the reason for this is that we (the Japanese) translated the words *manage* and *manager* as "control" and "controller." Translating it as "control" leads to "check and verify," but this is not what the real job of a manager is. The word *manage* has an element of "to do something well or easily," so "managing" means "doing something well and easily." One could say that the definition of a manager is "one who makes people do their job well in an easy way."

Managers get results from the work their people do. The manager's role is not to check people's work, but rather to liberally spend time seeing how people can do their work faster, more easily, and more accurately. The manager in the Toyota Production System workplace has to focus on the most important thing to help those who are adding value. That is the elimination of waiting, transportation, and inspection and increasing the ratio of processing to other activities—in other words, creating flow. The role of the manager is to create an environment in which flow can advance for the people who work there. What do we mean by "an environment in which flow can advance"?

We're not asking the manager to think up new equipment or new jigs and get someone to make them—although that would be helpful, it will be a lot faster to do it within the current organization structure, since we want to develop people as much as possible within that existing structure.

The more important thing is to create a structure in which people can actually think about and ponder the strategy set by management, plan its implementation, and actually carry it out in a concrete way. We need to develop a group that can take improvement ideas. If that group can make the ideas that are given to them by the shop floor concrete quickly and by themselves, then a lot more ideas will be forthcoming from the shop floor. That, in turn, will create an action-oriented work environment that will definitely move in the direction of flow.

One mistake that people often make is feeling that you can just make the plan and then wait for the reports to come in.

What's required is that you check to make sure people can carry it out. If they don't understand, think of better ways to explain it. If you don't get the results you wanted, then you may have to get into the thick of things and work up a sweat on the shop floor yourself.

Here are some examples of concrete actions that you as a manager can take to increase flow in your area.

- If processes are physically separated, move them together and do one-piece flow between them.
- Keep adding machines to the flow until you can make a complete finished good in a one-piece flow.
- Make a first-in, first-out finished goods storage and when what is necessary for today's production has been made, stop the line.
- Do the same thing for other part manufacturing lines.

To learn how to join lines and processes, please read Ohno's teachings in Lesson 6 of Chapter 1: "The Foreman or Leader Is the One Who 'Breaks' the Standard." When Ohno was able to reduce the headcount of the production line by making improvements, he took out the best person, who then helped join the processes of the next line. As they kept increasing the flow between processes, they freed up more people, who then became the "catching bowl" for all the kaizen ideas.

First, take your time and really build up the first line. Once you start moving to other lines, you may find that some people can now make simple equipment. The kaizen team and the line leader will get more excited and have more ability to perform with every new line you add. They actually start looking forward to coming to work. Up to this point, however, they do need the support and help of management.

We are building up an environment in which flow can advance step by step. The next major step is to give management responsibility and authority to the areas that have improved their performance. Issues that a manager in a production environment has to deal with are always popping up. Giving up certain management responsibilities makes the manager's job more efficient and also gives people a chance to increase their skills. Developing people who can be trusted and delegated to and giving them the authority as well makes for a nice action-oriented workplace.

Once flow gets to a certain level, the next big issue is normally stoppages caused by equipment breakdowns. Once you have a line with one-piece flow, whether you like it or not, you'll notice a lot more equipment problems than you saw before. At this stage, we want to focus our efforts on creating an environment that can accommodate a strong maintenance structure. If every little breakdown results in a stoppage, we will have larger financial problems, so at first, this will mean getting insurance (extra inventory) in the right places to cover for the equipment stoppages. Don't rush to eliminate inventory. If you do, and a machine breakdown causes the whole line to shut down, the Toyota Production System you are putting in will lose everyone's support.

In the Toyota Production System, the parts will move many times faster than they do in a typical batch and queue system. In order to keep up with this speed, the most important thing is fast action on equipment problems. I highly encourage you to get this capability in-house instead of relying on contractors.

Another issue that will appear will be the problems of defects. This does not mean that the new system created these problems, but rather that they were always there and people were working on things that were unprofitable and even working up a sweat doing it. Things like reducing the number of setup parts that we have to sacrifice to get the right adjustments can be a great project for our new maintenance team.

Other issues will be that people feel that inventory is moving faster and there may be more part shortages, which will make it seem that problem solving is getting more difficult than it was with the previous way of doing things. (Things are not being processed faster, but since there is less safety stock, it will feel as if they are moving faster.) If we keep solving issues at the speed we used to, it will be too slow. We need to create an environment in which faster problem and issue resolution can take place. Once our maintenance team and structure are in place, we can focus on reducing breakdowns and transportation.

Things You Can Do to Reduce Equipment Breakdowns
- Foundational maintenance training
- Keeping a record of what went wrong and what fixes were put in place
- Reduction of changeover time
- Working on a preventive maintenance schedule
- Understanding the conditions required for good parts
- Understanding how to find issues when they are still small

Things You Can Do to Reduce Transportation

- Joining processes
- Making a replenishment type of line
- Changing the layout
- Reducing the processing time

There will be many jobs that have to be done to create the environment we want, but we can't do them all at once. Just do one at a time. "Profit comes while pursuing flow" was mentioned in Chapter 1. We could also say that small frequent transportation is like healthy blood, which transports nutrients to the cells and takes away the waste products. We can be quite sure that as we pursue one-piece flow, the blood goes through small capillaries to cells that didn't get blood before, and naturally things that didn't start to move start gaining movement ability.

I am sure you will agree with me that rather than having management tell people in detail what is wrong with their areas and how to fix them, it is a lot more motivational for them to fix things on their own while pursuing flow.

I ask managers everywhere to take off their "control" hat and put on their "I make it easy for my people to work" hat, and then work hard at that new job.

Giving Authority: Growing People You Can Empower

A long time ago, the words, "Leave it up to the shop floor" were commonplace. In this kind of workplace, while management was there, it could not exercise any authority over production. If the people in the workplace got offended in any way, then the work would slow down or stop, so the only thing that management in these places could do was "leave it up to the shop floor."

Also, the skills of the workers weren't always based on logic or sound engineering, but rather on "making things happen" in the conditions they were given, largely based on experience.

When you leave it up to a supervisor who should not be given authority, sooner or later you run into the following problems:

- The manager soon loses his understanding of the workplace and has to "leave it up to the workers."
- The manager thinks that she can manage using numbers and graphs and gets out of touch with the actual workplace.
- If the results aren't forthcoming, people are pushed to make it happen.
- Motivation of the workforce goes down.
- The workplace becomes "weak" or unable to deal with changes.

In other words, we are back to the "olden days" where we had no choice but to leave it up to the "guys who are working there."

When I talk about "giving authority to the workplace," I am not talking about going back to the old way of doing things. In a Toyota Production System environment, if you cannot move the authority to make decisions and carry them out to the shop floor or workplace level, many elements will not be able to function properly.

Because of this, we have no choice but to develop supervisors whom we can transfer authority to. The first step is relentless standardization so that we can tell whether something is OK or not OK.

Standardization All the Way

In a production setting, it is practically impossible to have the same conditions for people, things, equipment, jigs and tools, and product at all times. Even equipment wears down and starts changing. It's hard to see these changes from day to day, isn't it? The same person may feel fine in the morning, but be under the weather in the afternoon. If he is worrying about something that is taking his mind off work, then the risk of having some kind of problem escalates significantly. The damage from a problem happening won't be too bad, though, if most of the conditions are within tolerance.

There are many, many change points (things that could change and affect our work) in the workplace, and it is impossible for the supervisor or manager to check up on each one all the time. The best way to combat this situation is to determine standards that have as wide a scope as possible and are as detailed as possible. Here are the main things that we should have standards for.

Standard work. Do the work the way the supervisor decided it should be done.

Work instructions. These are the step-by-step instructions and the key points needed to maintain quality, safety, and speed.

Work explanation sheets. There should be many of these. Complicated jobs like doing a changeover, changing the cutting tools, and doing a quality check all need explanation sheets.

Other Standards

Production control boards

Box for holding the production kanbans

Call for help andon

Marked areas to keep the pallets of raw materials or
incoming parts

Marked area for the different finished goods according
to product number

Shelves of maintenance spare parts inventory for each
machine

The manager's role is to have the supervisor create standards that will minimize the chances of abnormalities happening. By making this visual, one can see whether the group members are sticking to the standards they made and agreed to. If there is an issue, the manager can call the supervisor using the call andon so that everyone learns, "We stop when we find that something strange is going on." (Stop when things are abnormal.)

For the supervisor, we have her check to make sure that people are doing the work in the standard way. If they are not, then she teaches them until they understand and makes them do it the standard way. We want to ensure that work is always done in accordance with the agreed-upon standard.

So the first step in transferring authority to the workplace is the creation of standards and the deployment of them using the jidoka (stop and fix) method. This way, both the manager and the supervisor will have the same standards inside their heads. We have now created a structure in which the manager will be able to say, "I have given them full authority, and I know they are doing it the correct way."

The Supervisor Makes the Standards, Checks to See if the Standards Are Followed, and Teaches People How to Follow the Standards if They Are Not Doing So

Up to now, I have used the word *supervisor* to mean the leader right under the manager. Underneath the supervisor will be a team leader. As we saw in Ohno's teachings in Chapter 1, Lesson 6, the role of the team leader is to "break the standard." I told you the history of how that happened, but since this role is very important, I want to add a few more thoughts concerning it.

Ohno had the best people improve their areas, and when this allowed him to free up a person, he took out those best people and had them do more improvements. These people were not working in the line, but were working with people in the line to improve their area. This is a lot different from the way we use team leaders now. I strongly believe that we need to remember why this position was created in the first place, and no matter what, have a person who can focus on improvement in every workshop.

"People who break the standard" is quite a strong phrase, but it means a group of people who will find a better way of doing things. The team leader is the person who pulls the team together. There is no need to teach someone who has skills and experience. He will know much more about the area than the manager or the supervisor ever will, since he lives with it day after day. So rather than training the team leader in details, the best thing to do is to give him "eyes to see improvement potential."

For example, make things flow: when things are not flowing, this leads to replacing tools during changeovers and lots of short stoppages in production. Once the reasons for these are identified and eliminated, we can reduce stoppages and increase flow.

- Make the work easier (ergonomics improvement)
- Make things last longer (tools and tooling life)

The team leader is there to break the standards created by the supervisor.

The manager teaches the supervisor how to deal with abnormal situations.

Even though we have now created a stable workplace with jidoka and standard work, we still cannot relax. As I said before, most of the Toyota style is based on replenishment or downstream pull production. There are two types of kanbans: withdrawal and production kanbans. In Toyota, these two types of kanbans are used to join all processes from assembly up to raw materials. The total amount of work in process is far less than that in a traditional batch and queue operation. Also, if one area stops operations and doesn't pull parts, all the processes before it soon stop. This is taking the jidoka concept into the pull system. (The system alerts people when there is a problem and ceases operation until that problem is solved.)

A defect or problem will soon affect the downstream processes, so the work of a production manager is very demanding. If she were to try to deal with all the issues by herself, there would not be enough time for her to do so. Because of flow and pull and managing with little inventory, the effects of problems in processing or unexpected incidents affect other areas much faster.

A good supervisor will be able to find the problem early and fix it, preventing the damage from having a large effect; however, we can't simply rely on the skills of the supervisor. Since we are in a pull system, the more pressing thing is that any and all downstream problems are noticed directly by the people working in the area, not by the supervisor or management. When management hears of an issue from the supervisor, the supervisor quite often doesn't know the full downstream picture at that time. If the supervisor has to wait for a management decision before he can take action, it will be too late.

When the supervisor hears a report from the downstream process about a problem and can confirm that it arose in his area, he will take a quick stopgap measure and at the same time will let management know what he has done as the immediate stopgap and what the effect on the downstream process has been.

If it is a product problem, then the supervisor will have the workers in his area check the quality of the product in finished goods storage. The supervisor himself will go to the manager, let her know what the problem is and what is being done about it, and then go to the downstream process and see how far the defect has flowed downstream. Once the defect is found, then all parts, including the parts in the supervisor's area, will be collected. Based on the information coming in from the people in his area, the supervisor, along with production scheduling and the downstream process, will decide how they will change the production schedule and manage the new one.

There isn't much that a supervisor or manager can do by herself, but by teaching people the "standard work in an emergency" and by developing supervisors and managers who can make the right decisions in emergency situations, the group is much better able to deal with these kinds of incidents.

By developing supervisors who can think the same way as the manager, we can feel safe in giving them large areas of control. Teaching the workers what to do when a problem arises and training supervisors to make management decisions is all part of giving authority to the shop floor. In other words, this includes developing supervisors who can have authority delegated to them.

Management training people under them is not the same as having them do things that are outside their authority. It is really working together. As a result, though, what you do together does become "pretraining" for management.

"Delegating authority," in Ohno's words, is "putting in sensory perceptions like a nervous system on the shop floor. A shop floor that is changing all the time."

Sharing "Out of Standard" Information

Managers must not only delegate authority. They must also create an environment where they can understand what is going on in the workplace. This will prevent them from "leaving it up to the guys." Andon boards, hour-by-hour charts, and a fixed number of kanban cards are all part of a system of sharing information. Some tools are visually displayed. The best use of these tools, however, is to foster communication and discussion between the management and the people working there. Just making things visual is not effective.

For example, the point of the hour-by-hour board is to have the supervisor visit the area once an hour, talk with the people working there about how things are going, thank them and encourage them, and, if there are issues, find out more about them. This short but regular communication becomes a great exchange of information leading to wonderful improvement ideas.

Convenient auto-updating boards do not provide a means of communication. Also, nothing will give you better information from the floor than communicating with the people who are working there. A manager who doesn't communicate, but just looks at numbers and then says, "We're not making it," isn't going to have many good ideas for improvement.

As a manager, motivate yourself to have conversations about the andons, the kanbans, and the finished goods store. As far as how to work with the finished goods storage is concerned, I will cover it in more detail in the section on making a line that motivates people.

Delegating authority to the workplace means developing supervisors who can be responsible and sharing the information about out-of-scope or abnormal situations.

Management Should Make Workplaces That Motivate People to Work and Sustain the Motivation

The thing that makes the manager happiest is having workers who are motivated to excel. What kind of management is needed to sustain this high motivation? Thinking, reading, getting training, fair evaluations, the right motivation scheme, feeling that one is growing, and being praised when they do well are all important. It's easy to say, but getting everyone to feel this way is very difficult.

I used to talk to people in a kindly way, shoot the breeze with them, and ask them, "Is there anything related to work that you are struggling with?" You may find this strange, but this "normal" management activity led to a huge mistake that I will never forget.

I was talking to an employee who was checking parts at the quality assurance station, and I asked him, "So is the time required for adjusting the machine after the changeover getting shorter?" He responded to me very sincerely, and we had a great conversation. I said, "Thank you," and left the place, but in the afternoon of that day, we had a defect from the area where this person was working.

This is just my guess, but this employee was probably not used to being talked to and was wondering whether he had answered my questions correctly or in the right way. He kept thinking about this, and that was the reason for his mistake. I had tried to be motivational, but I had actually wound up hurting him instead.

When I wrote about how top management should act and that it was OK to look at the workplace but to avoid talking to people, that learning came from this bitter experience. Some people like to get a smile and a punch in the shoulder, but I think it's best not to treat them too casually.

I also once overheard an engineer who was trying to work on how we could run a different variation of a chassis part through the production line say, "When we have many versions going through the same line and only one version has a design change, I need to test out all versions to see if it will still work. I am working hard, but all the conditions from the old versions don't make it easy for me to make the line work with the new version. Yes, we can now make a new version, but I was not able to make any improvements on the line," he complained.

The supervisor also chimed in. "Up to now, the jigs worked with the current production. You know, we forced them to accept the new version, so it really isn't as easy to use as it should be." Both the engineer who had to modify the equipment and the supervisor who had to use it were not happy with the extra complexity that they now had to deal with.

If we can understand what makes a production area "motivational" and what type of structure generates motivation, and add good management to that, then the motivation can be sustained. I used to think that good management came first and the motivation of the employees would follow, but I have seen that it is really difficult to sustain doing things that way. I have now come to the conclusion that setting up the area to be motivational comes first. It's a paradigm shift, much like downstream pull is a shift from the push method.

I then asked myself, "What are the conditions needed in a motivational workplace?" It's one in which everyone is thinking, "I can do this job better than anyone else, and I want people to notice it and to evaluate me based on it" as she works. A workplace that can achieve this must be structured in such a way that:

- It's easy to see how much effort a person is putting into the job.
- Everyone can see the results of the work.
- Everyone can see the results of changes and how they affect the output.

Actually, the shop floor lines in the Toyota Production System are very much in line with this kind of structure. Visual management, abnormality control, replenishment systems, production according to takt time, fixed quantity deliveries, just in time, one-piece flow, tsurube pull, and water spiders (water striders) have all been developed to make things easy to understand. These innovations help to:

- Show problems.
- Allow you to find issues fast.
- Reduce inventory.
- Reduce lead time.
- Grow and develop people.

I will deal with each method separately, but when good management is combined with all these methods, the switch is pushed on and the payback in results is multiplied. Making a work area that keeps on motivating people is a huge part of a manager's job.

Downstream Pull/Replenishment Line

As has been stated many times, the most important thing in the Toyota Production System is the concept of *flow*. But flow by itself is not enough. One must properly incorporate a downstream pull and replenishment structure to reduce overproduction and get to an effective just-in-time method (see Figure 3-1).

The supervisor is like a store or supermarket manager who has been given a retail business to manage. The store manager is responsible for the profit and loss for her supermarket. When you visit a supermarket, you can see the effectiveness and motivation of management just by looking at how much finished goods storage the supermarket has. If there are any problems with processes, things, people, or equipment, that manager will have to keep lots of inventory. If there isn't much inventory, then you can assume that the manager's kaizen efforts are working out well.

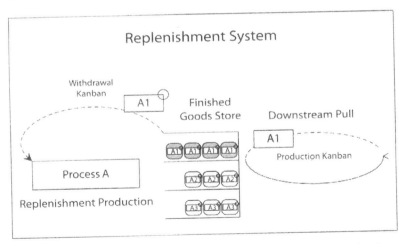

Figure 3-1 You can see how much effort the team members are putting into improvement by viewing the finished goods store.

So the true picture of both how well one is managing and the skill level of the team in that area is visible at the finished goods store, and therefore people will naturally want to compete with the others so that they don't look bad. Even if the skill level and assets are the same, good or bad management can have a big effect on the results. That is what the store can show you. Whenever I need to visit a company, I always start by looking at the finished goods storage. That pretty much tells me most of what I need to know about the place, including how driven to excel the management team is.

Also, since we are working in a downstream pull environment, the problems and issues of the downstream processes are also visible. The extent to which these issues can be corrected is largely determined by the leadership, technique, and collaboration and adjustment skills with other departments.

Basically, for the person in charge of an area, if he has an unmanaged finished goods store, it becomes blatantly obvious to everyone that he is a bad manager, he has no skill, and he also has no motivation to improve. Once you understand that, you can't let things go on the way they are. You can't reduce inventory right away, but as the department improves, the inventory can be lowered. What's also critical is that when people see a reduction in the line's store inventory, the supervisor in charge of the line is praised for it and it positively affects his evaluation, as a correct judgment should.

A good image is the supervisor using the production control board, teaching, growing, encouraging, and making a workplace good at both offense and defense. The line now says, "We are managing ourselves, even at such low store levels." Basically, the inventory asset that was kept in the store has now changed to the skill level asset of the people in the line. Confidence gained this way will surely help with the next round of kaizen.

So our inventory asset has now changed into an asset of people's skill. The supervisor, engineer, and workers were given a spark of motivation, and that, combined with the supervisor's skill at developing people and her technical and managerial skills, was used to change the inventory asset into something that is not as easily measurable but much more useful.

My sincere wish is that you take these new assets so that you are always one step ahead and have a winning team.

The details of how we reduced the store inventory can be understood by going to the production control board. You should go to the board at least once an hour and talk to the workers. Ask them how the last hour went, have them reflect on the last hour, and then encourage them for the next hour. This kind of simple conversation will establish trust and lead to lots of good improvement ideas. Conversations that lead to improvement ideas won't come out of an automatic digital control board that counts the production for you. There is no need to talk for a long time, and you don't need to ask the workers how they were able to do it. Just using the hourly talk to thank them for their work and encourage them for the next hour is enough. This will also serve as a good example to the other "storekeepers" around you. Talk to the workers based on the production control board and everyone will benefit.

Sometimes people say, "It's a waste of time for workers to have to write down numbers on the production control board." These people believe that it is better to get one extra unit of production than to write things down on the board, and they automate the production control boards. However, if you approach the production control board and your team members with warmth and a personal touch, it will pay you a lot more dividends than free labor for one part day.

It is not a waste for employees to fill in the production control boards (see Figures 3-2 and 3-3). That is the start of conversations that beget improvement ideas.

Management and the supervisor having a conversation in front of the store for the line and the supervisor and the

Figure 3-2 The time it takes for employees to write things down is not wasted. It is the start of a good conversation that leads to improvement.

LINE A Production Control Board

September 17, 2014

Cable Assembly

Daily Requirement **450** Pc/Day		**Takt Time**	**60** Sec/Pc	

Operating Time	Planned Target / Cum.	**Actual** Target / Cum.	Comment	Times Andon Pulled	Working Schedule - Check
8:40 ₹ 9:30 (50min)	50 / 50	48 / 48	Maintenance by the operator 8:40~Start of the shift		Tom ✓
9:30 ₹ 10:40 (60min)	60 / 110	58 / 106	*Break (10:00~10:10) 10 min Cap falling at the insertion process Spring supply error	II	Tom ✓
10:40 ₹ 11:40 (60min)	60 / 170	60 / 166			Tom ✓
11:40 ₹ 13:25 (60min)	60 / 230	56 / 222	*Lunch Break (12:00~12:45) 45 min Line downtime for maintenance	III	Tom ✓
13:25 ₹ 14:25 (60min)	60 / 290	60 / 282			Tom ✓
14:25 ₹ 15:35 (60min)	60 / 350	57 / 339	*Break (15:00~15:10) 10 min Adjust play	I	Tom ✓
15:35 ₹ 16:35 (60min)	60 / 410	56 / 395		III	Tom ✓
16:35 ₹ 17:15 (40min)	40 / 450	32 / 427	*5 5 (17:15~17:25) 10 min Adjust play Grease can exchange	III	Tom ✓
17:15 ₹ Overtime Work (min)	/	23 / 450	Overtime work 30 min		Tom ✓

Line Stop Items	1: Changeover ·Adjustments 2: Defects 3: Frequent stop ·Equipment failure ·Maintenance	4: Plan downtime 5: No kanban	# of Defects :

Figure 3-3 Talking with the operator in front of the production control board inspires a "can do" mindset and is the start of finding improvement opportunities.

workers having a conversation in front of the production control board are what breathes life into the downstream pull production system. Challenge yourselves to do this so that you have a living management and create a fulfilling, exciting, and action-oriented workplace for everyone.

Dedicated Replenishment Lines

A dedicated replenishment line is a downstream pull line that makes things based on the pull from the downstream processes. "Dedicated" means that it makes only one product or part. The definition of a multiproduct line would be one that makes two or more types of things that require changeovers.

There are a lot of pros and cons that people look at in deciding whether to make something on a dedicated line or a multiproduct line, but generally speaking, if it is the same car, but with a different number of gears or a different shaft diameter, we would make it on the same line. This is still a dedicated line because even though the parts that go in are different, they are all made to takt time. If they cannot be made to takt time in the line, then they would be made on a subline.

At Toyota, we say, "Make things to takt time." Takt time is found by taking the required production for the day and determining how much time you will take to make one part. Takt time is one of the three elements of standard work. (The others are work sequence and standard work in process.) It's used not only to make the monthly plan for required labor, but also to make level production (heijunka), which creates the overall harmony of the plant. It is one of the most important aspects of the Toyota Production System.

If what we are making is basically the same automobile, the takt time is the same for all of them, so we can collect the lines that make the parts for the car and make them all at the same takt (pace) as the main assembly line. In other words, we can have production lines based on different products.

The good points of dedicated lines are that they are simple, and that it is easy to understand what is going on.

- Simple equipment with minimal investment to just do what is required
- Fewer equipment breakdowns because the lines are simple and don't have unnecessary features
- Compact equipment that uses space wisely and efficiently
- Fewer changeovers mean stable quality
- Kaizen activities can easily add automation, and productivity can increase
- The employees' kaizen skills will increase
- Shorter lead times

The key point of a successful dedicated line is to make the equipment simple, slim, compact, and low-cost.

In order to do this, it is imperative that we learn how to make our own equipment. The reason why I am a strong believer in making one's own equipment is the following: it is obvious that a company should control its own core technology, but if you can add to that by making equipment that doesn't exist anywhere else, you can really make use of your core skills and engineering. The other good thing about making equipment yourself is that every time you make something, new ideas are incorporated into the equipment. The engineers' motivation increases, and as a result you are now well on your way toward "simple, slim, compact, and low-cost" equipment. Let's compare this to production lines that can accommodate multiple products, which we will call *all-purpose* lines.

Presses and casting, forging, and molding activities pretty much operate in an all-purpose line environment. No businessman will put these machines, which cost lots of money, in a dedicated line.

To achieve the goal of making things to takt time, the dedicated line is obviously the better of the two. But because of constraints on technology, engineering skills, and equipment, there are still many all-purpose lines remaining. Most of the people working in this environment probably think that this situation is the way things will always be.

In the machinery production engineering department at Toyota, the rule was that you had to do a changeover for each kanban on the all-purpose lines. The evaluation of the all-purpose line and investment decisions were made not based on a comparison with the dedicated line, but rather on machine utilization and engineering constraints. The best way to look at an all-purpose line is to view it as a "management problem to be solved."

There are many processes that have to be done with large-scale equipment because of engineering limitations, but I strongly believe that down the road, with innovation in processing, simple lines will be possible. The world is full of examples of small equipment that used to be a lot larger.

Further Development and Innovation on Dedicated Lines

Many companies that use small, dedicated equipment to get better results have a history of making their own machines. An in-house machine-making department is encouraging to production engineers as they work hard to master new processes. The managers support them, helping them make useful equipment and taking the time to hear updates from them on how things are going. By the way, during these updates, it's best not to ask too many detailed questions, but rather to just say, "We are really looking forward to what you guys come up with, and we believe in you. Good job." If the group members hear questions like, "Did you analyze this?" or, "What if you did it this way?" they may feel that they have to do this because a top manager told them to, and this will needlessly delay the timetable for the new piece of equipment.

To all you senior managers out there, "Your young people are a lot smarter than you are. Give them the authority to figure things out!" If you can do that, when they do succeed in making their machine, they will gain a huge amount of satisfaction and the company will get a lot of great assets in the process. (I'm talking less about machines and more about "can-do" people.)

Companies that figure out new processing methods and equipment can often take the cost of doing something down tenfold. Huge cost reductions become possible when you change the equipment that does the work.

Many companies make the same kinds of parts, all of which may have different takt times, in a multipart production line and make them at a very fast pace. Every time the company needs to make a new product, it will adjust the line a little bit, and where extra capacity is needed, it will add a new piece of equipment. This is how production lines get complex. The thinking is, "I'm using existing equipment, so the more new parts I can throw on this line, the lower the cost will be." The accounting-based illusion of cost reduction makes it very hard to get away from this way of thinking.

However, as time passes, equipment becomes older, the mechanisms for joining the processes get worn down, and one day you will have to take out the old equipment and put a new piece of expensive machinery in its place. I have firsthand experience with this, and it really is not motivating at all to work hard to introduce new parts or products into such a line.

We really want to give our engineers the joy of using new equipment and new methods to produce the new products, and we want to incorporate the new ideas that we have had into our new line. That is motivating.

On the flip side, engineers are prone to be "catalog engineers," just lining up expensive pieces of machinery that they can find in the marketplace. Because of this, top management must keep reminding them of simple, slim, compact, low cost, and short lead times. Encourage them to pursue these goals in their new lines, and let them feel that each time they make a new line; they are increasing their skills as well as increasing the company's manufacturing bench strength.

You know you are well on the way to success when you hear words like, "Hey, what are you going to do next?" or, "What are you guys making now?" throughout the company. That atmosphere is fun and motivating for everyone!

Clear Straight Flow

It used to be that at banks, train ticket windows, and hotels, when there were three windows at which to purchase, there would be three lines leading up to them, but now the general idea is to have one line and have people go to the next space that opens up.

When we still had to line up at a particular window, you would see the other lines moving faster, and you would be upset at your bad luck and the slowness of the line you were in. (In some countries' airports, we still have this situation, especially in the customs and immigration areas.)

While the single line does seem to have solved many problems, it has only spread the delay in the line more evenly for everyone; it has not really increased the speed at which the line is working or processing requests. Because of this, we cannot honestly say that this has solved the key issue. In fact, we are now less able to determine whether the delay is caused by the person's work at the window or whether it has more to do with the customer.

If the line gets really long, help may arrive, but basically it is in an unmanaged state. The customers at least don't have to deal with the feeling of, "I wonder if the next line would be faster," but that's about the only good thing. From the customers' point of view, there still is a lot of waiting time associated with the line. From the employees' point of view, no matter how hard they work, they really can't make a big difference in the number of people waiting, and so it's difficult to fairly evaluate their hard work.

This methodology (one line for multiple windows) is something that I do not recommend in a production facility;

however, I see many companies managing queues this way. If this is allowed to continue, the production line and also the relationships of the people who work there will start to experience many problems.

Why is this not a good idea? Let me give you an actual example (see Figure 3-4).

There were three production lines, each manned by two people, that could make the same parts. It was necessary to do a changeover when different parts had to be made. Once the team had made one product, it would then take the next production kanban for the group and make that. If production on one line was delayed, then the people and lines that depended on this line for product would face a shortage, and the overall production of the facility would be negatively affected.

The production kanbans that feed the three lines are really the same as the people lining up in a bank with many tellers. If one line has a delay, then the work orders are concentrated in the other two lines. The harder the other two lines work, the more jobs they have to do. Even though they are working hard, they still have only two-thirds of the total production capacity, so they will have to work overtime. Even if one of the lines isn't stopped for the whole day, minor stoppages and defects will delay the group for a specific amount of time.

There are other problems, too. When the teams see the jobs lined up on the kanban board, they see some jobs that are easy to do and other jobs that are harder to do. This makes them think, "I don't want to do two hard jobs in a row," which then leads to subtle timing games to avoid the hard jobs. As a result, this group was always doing two hours of overtime a day.

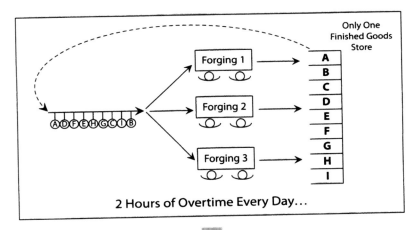

Clear Flow

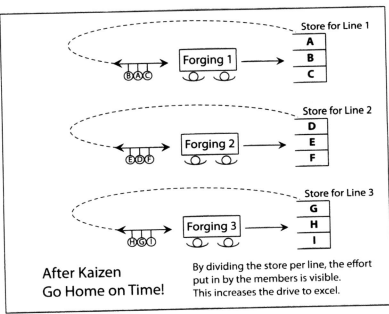

Figure 3-4 Separating the store for each line makes the effort put in by the team members visible. This increases the drive to excel.

In the Toyota method, we changed this to decide which products each line would make and separated the finished goods area for each line. Just by doing that, in a minimal amount of time, improvements started to happen, and the teams had less overtime. We even started seeing entries in the daily log like, "We finished our production early today, so we helped out the other line by taking two of its kanbans." The teams also started to discuss the problematic products with one another and made changes to make the changeovers easier.

All that changed was the following, but they made all the difference.

1. It was easy to see the effects of "working hard."
2. It was easy to see the production volume of each line.
3. The company listened to the teams' improvement ideas.

We did not try to force a competition, but everyone wants to show that she is doing a better job than those on the other teams. When we created an environment in which this feeling could flourish, the teams started thinking about improvements, and this led to better teamwork between the teams as well. I really felt how wonderful it is to have good teamwork when I experienced this.

The results that these lines achieved started bringing in many "tourists" to the area, who then influenced the people and the production areas around them. A little drop in the pond had made big waves throughout the organization.

This methodology is called the *clear flow method*, where each line has predetermined products that it makes, and therefore, its capacity, flow, and also improvements become obvious to everyone. I also have previously mentioned this, but don't forget to use the production management board.

Create a good structure and add good management to it to make a workplace that can make full use of people's skill, improvement ideas, and teamwork. I think you can see that this is quite possible and not that difficult to do.

High-Frequency Pull

The kanbans coming in from the customer are like production instructions for our own operations. So how should one take the information from the customer and give it to the shop floor in a way that will encourage kaizen?

First of all, one could take all the orders that need to go into one truckload, separate them by product numbers, and give them to the lines in a "one-truckload chunk" of orders. When Toyota started working on the kanban system with its suppliers, this is how most of those suppliers did it, and many of them continue to use this method to this day. We call this *ship set production*. We make all the parts that will go on the truck, and all of those parts will be sent to the shipping area, where they are staged as one truckload and then loaded on the truck. So we are pulling per truckload, or a truckload pull. The good point is that we can combine certain jobs so that we can work in a batch or a pattern that minimizes changeovers.

The finished goods storage area for each line will have lots of finished goods sitting around before the pull for the truck, and hardly any inventory after the pull. If we choose this method, it will be very hard to see how well the management is doing its job by looking at the finished goods store. This is now a line where if you work hard at improving, it is hard to see the fruits of your labor, and it will also be hard for management to give a fair evaluation of the employees working there.

The other method will be to pull one kanban's worth of parts from the finished goods area and then to start production on one kanban's worth of parts. In the Toyota group, we have improved our logistics functions so that we can do this. We call this the *high-frequency pull* method. It will not be efficient to pull one kanban's worth of goods from one line, so one logistics person will look after several lines. He will make a round every 10 or 15 minutes, going around the area and pulling finished goods from the different lines (parts) at each bus stop.

When the logistics person takes away the finished goods, he will take the kanban attached to the goods that he just picked and give it back to the production line. This then becomes the production kanban. The production line will then produce in the sequence in which it gets the kanbans. In this case, we will get a group of kanbans from the customer, but we will put the kanbans in a sequence for the production lines and go pick each one that was finished.

In order to be able to do this kind of production, it is essential that the changeovers from one type of production to another can be done very fast and easily and within the kanban replenishment time.

Since we've already got to this point, let's put in an hourly production control board where the manager of the line and the people who work there can talk about what went well and what needs improvement. It's equally important to talk about the successes, such as why are we able to work with much less inventory now and what was the key activity that we did to accomplish this. The manager then needs to thank the team and make sure that the activity is counted toward them. If people don't feel that their hard work is appreciated, there is no real reward for those transporting the parts in the high-frequency method.

There are many benefits to doing a high-frequency pull, but the main ones are:

- We can know the status of the production line in real time.
- We can see how good a job the manager of the line is doing.

By accomplishing these things, people are more motivated and kaizen change for good starts happening on its own.

Teaching people what high-frequency pull is and saying, "Do high-frequency pull" is not enough for success. Without having a mechanism allowing the hard work that people do to be evaluated visually and appreciated, the only benefit you will get will be less work in process. Please don't forget that the real benefit of high-frequency pull is to coax out the motivation of the manager and the workers on that line.

If your company is still doing a truckload pull, it means that you are ignoring the hard work of your people and your managerial staff. If we can easily see the hard work that people put in and can compare the different lines, everyone naturally wants to say, "How can we do it better?" If you can keep this at the forefront of your deployment, I highly recommend high-frequency pull as a tool to motivate your people to make more improvements and at a faster pace.

CHAPTER 4

IF YOU RESPECT OTHER PEOPLE, THEY WILL TRUST YOU

want to say a few words to those of us who will be head of an operation in a foreign country. I do this because I really want you to be successful in deploying the Toyota Production System, both in your own company and in your suppliers and partners in that country.

For those of you who are well traveled and think, "I know what it's like in this country," this chapter is especially for you. I think you will get a deeper understanding because of your experiences to date.

I can also say that I see more failures among those who have just enough experience to think that they are "experienced." When you are in the country on a business trip, you are still there as a guest. Since you are not going to be there forever, even if you offend your local partners and fellow employees, they will smile and put up with you while you are there. Don't confuse the "success" you had in the country while you were a guest with experience living and working in that country.

Talk to the Top People and Other Expatriates About Their Experience

Once you know that you will be working in a different country, visit the expatriate who was the previous head of the operation. You will be able to get lots of useful information from that person. It's also important that you talk to people who have worked in countries other than the one where you will be working. You will be able to hear other stories of things to watch out for. You will probably be quite surprised by how much difference there is among different countries. Because the country is different, the rules and structure will be different as well.

Of course we need to obey the local laws, but there are also cultural norms that have developed over the years. Even if something is not written down as law, there are many things that one should not do in a particular country. Some countries don't like the OK sign or the thumbs-up sign. In some countries, it is bad luck if you bring money to weddings in odd-number amounts, the way we do in Japan. Things that you are doing with goodwill in your heart are sometimes taken the wrong way, and it really hurts when you realize that you have unwittingly offended or embarrassed someone.

I don't want to scare people who are going overseas, but I want you to know that there will be differences from Japanese practice, so learn what they are from people who have experience in that country. Then, please become a person who can see differences and understand them. If possible, understand where those differences come from and why people think a certain way. You will now understand the source of that country's thinking.

If the people think, "Our new boss is really good this time," it helps increase the value of the company brand name. You are probably there for only three to five years, so the first impression you give will be very important.

Think of Managing an Overseas Plant as a Three-Story Building

After you have heard many stories and learned from others' experiences, keep the metaphor of a three-story building in your mind when you're managing overseas operations. I was taught this by another person who had had overseas experience. I hope it is helpful to you (see Figure 4-1).

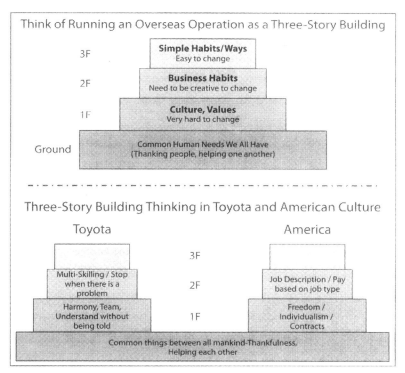

Figure 4-1 Think of running an overseas operation as a three-story building.

Ground level. These are the needs that everyone has: thanking and being thanked, helping one another out, and so on.

Level 1. This level involves culture and values—these are very hard to change.

Level 2. This level deals with business habits and ways of doing things. It is not impossible to change them, but you do have to be smart about making the change.

Level 3. These are simple habits and ways. They can be quite easy to change.

If you want to change something that is on the first floor, it will be very hard for people to accept. For example, in the United States, the concepts that most people value most are freedom and liberty. In Japan, we are more harmony-oriented; we also value "holding out your hand to help," and we judge people as part of a team. When it comes to communication, we (the Japanese) think in ways like, "You should know without being told."

We tend to think of Americans as being selfish and always looking at contracts, and they see us as caring too much about harmony, which is not easy for them to accept.

Given this situation, telling the Americans, "Let's value harmony" and making that a critical element of the Toyota Production System is not going to work. If you think, "Valuing harmony is critical to getting the TPS to work, so we will work on that," you are now talking about changing something on the first floor of the building, which will be hard to do and will take forever. That will result in the response, "It's not possible to do that here."

Concepts like job rotation and multiskilling may also be difficult to introduce, but these are more second-floor concepts. You don't have to change the first floor for this. You can be smart about it, use the wisdom of the local people, and make it happen.

The person who taught me about the three-story building was in the United States. He told me a story about developing a culture of rotating jobs in the United States. The normal situation, he told me, was that when one person was promoted, the others who had been considered for the promotion but didn't get it often left the company. They were good people, so their leaving was a big loss to the company. He thought, "Wouldn't it be nice if we could just rotate people into different jobs the way we do in Japan, so that they don't have to leave?" He talked to the HR director in the United States, and she said, "Why not see if anyone will volunteer to rotate jobs?" When volunteers were asked for, there were a few managers who said that they wouldn't mind doing another job, so he had them move to a different responsibility. This was something very rare in the United States, and so many people were watching to see how it would work out. Once they saw that the first group liked it and that it was working out well, many others started to volunteer to rotate jobs, and then it became the new norm.

The Americans also told this person that one thing that was unacceptable to them was "looking over someone's shoulder." If you give a person the responsibility, let him handle it. Also, you must be very protective of people's privacy. These are first-floor items, and we cannot go in those areas with our Japanese mentality.

Another large obstacle to creating flow was the many different job grades in the United States. There were many job grades in even the assembly part of the U.S. automotive world, and different job grades meant different pay scales. Given this situation, asking people to be more multiskilled and rotate jobs was quite hard. So to make flow and to do multiprocess handling, the U.S. HR directors talked with the people and the union to reduce the number of job grades. It took a while, but in the end it was understood to be a good thing.

Apparently, "stop the line when you see a problem" also took a long time to get used to in the U.S. business culture. Everyone knew how expensive it was to shut the line down, so they were really afraid to do it. It took a lot of discussion and smarts to get people to understand that they would not be fired if they stopped the line and that showing and reporting problems was a good thing.

Another thing that was difficult, but that in the end proved possible to change, was the concept that even though your job content changed based on how many cars were being made that month, your monthly salary would not change. Of course, one would be paid overtime if one worked overtime. Taiichi Ohno had the same struggles in the 1940s and 1950s with the idea that "I should be paid more if we are making more." It took a lot of explanation and creativity, I'm sure, to overcome this thinking in the United States, which had a long history of manufacturing.

Different job grades and stopping the line when you see a problem are second-floor items. They are not easily changed, but it is possible to change them if you are creative in the approach you use. That approach should not be pushed by the Japanese, but should be developed by listening to the local people and pulling good ideas through them. In order for you to be successful, the local staff members have to understand what you are trying to do. The best thing is to explain in very clear terms and use many examples. I will talk about how to do that in more detail at a later point.

I think that if you can think of the three-story building, it will allow you to work with the local population without any major hiccups. Of course, this is a lot easier said than done. Many of us will spend years just trying to understand what exactly is on the first floor—the things that we should not touch. Even after spending many years in a country, there is no guarantee that you will "get it."

When one starts traveling down the Toyota method toward flow, many of the current management methods are not adequate anymore. That means that the rules and structure have to change. Without knowing it, you may try to address something that is on the first floor.

For example, you have three employees who were paid for piecework before, and now you want to make them into a three-person team doing things in a one-piece-flow method. Obviously, the payment scheme will have to change. The employees are quite concerned about how they are paid, so the change needs to be implemented quickly. You will need some professional advice as to whether the new method is legal in that country, and even if it is legal, gaining acceptance from the affected employees is a totally different matter. Such challenges will arise frequently.

Even people who have been in the country for a long time will make mistakes, so the best thing for you to do is not to be directly involved at first. Instead of you making the decision, get some local staff members as your team. Every time an issue comes up, you can get them together, explain the goal or the direction you want to go in, and have them come up with an idea or method that will work. They should also be the ones to explain the decision to the other employees.

If such a thing does not exist, create a formal "Presidential Strategy Group," explain only the goal or purpose of the major issue, and let the local people figure out how they will do that. You need to give up authority to this group. By doing this, you'll avoid talk like, "There's a Japanese guy who knows nothing who is making us do stupid things and having us follow some crazy rules." Instead, you will now have a method that is in harmony with the local customs and ways of doing things.

A different kind of hard work will be needed if you are going overseas in the preparation stage, but if you are going there as the top person after an operation has been running for several years or a decade or so, the various methods and rules that were put in place when the site was started are probably out of date, as markets and the country's development status have changed. These gaps are evident in many countries. This is especially true in the HR area, and even more so in the way top management is paid, promoted, and retired. Updating these rules and procedures to reflect the current reality is a must. Accept this task as something that you must do as the top manager, talk to your presidential staff, and get through these difficult issues. Please do not put them on the back burner for the next person to solve. The longer these problems and issues fester, the harder it will be to change them. Many Japanese companies fall into this unfortunate situation.

To summarize, many things that you may think are difficult can actually be accomplished quite easily, and many things that seem simple to do are very difficult to make happen. Don't keep thinking about those issues yourself—talk to your local staff; see if they are issues that are on the first, second, or third floor; and make the changes accordingly.

Make an Environment Where It's OK to Say, "I'm Sorry"

Japan is probably the only country where if someone makes a mistake, he will say, "I messed up; I'm sorry. It's my responsibility." In other countries, where the workers are not as respected, making a mistake often means losing one's job. That means that no one will own up to or admit mistakes, and that people will hide their friends' mistakes, too. That thinking hasn't changed much over the years. In Japan, the ability to say, "I'm sorry" is taken as a good thing, but in most countries this is not so.

The other way of understanding the Toyota Production System is as "abnormality management," so guessing what the root cause of a problem is and guessing what the solution should be is not going to work. Unless we can develop a culture in which the workers can admit mistakes without being negatively affected, the Toyota Production System will not take root.

In a Japanese company, if one makes a mistake, the concept that "you will be forgiven if you honestly admit it" is generally taken as a given. Even so, some managers will evaluate an employee negatively for making mistakes, and others may think, "I need to punish this person; otherwise I cannot keep the integrity of our rules," and so will create a destructive atmosphere that leads to walls of separation between people and will hurt the overall operations of the company. This even happens quite frequently in Japan—how much more elsewhere!

So this concept of creating a culture in which one can say, "I'm sorry" is very difficult. That is not a reason not to identify problems, not to do root cause analysis, and not to fix anything, though. That is an option that we do not have.

One option that we do have is to not care about the words "I'm sorry," but just be able to do root cause analysis on the real problem. What seems to be effective is to say, "When a problem happens, you don't have to apologize, but please do recurrence prevention to ensure that the same problem does not happen again."

However, the words *recurrence prevention* are also really not commonly used outside Japan, so getting this concept understood will take some time. In many companies, the workers' job, the managers' job, and the support staff's job are all well defined, so when a defect occurs, there is a person whose job it is to fix that defect, and if she fixes that defect in the standard way, that is the end of the problem.

Recurrence prevention is not an easy concept to teach, but I think it can take root in the company a lot more easily than, "I'm sorry." During your weekly management meetings, you will get reports on the operations. When one of the managers really gets into the root cause and does recurrence prevention, make sure to say, "Thank you so much for doing such a good job on recurrence prevention." I think it starts with your saying, "Thank you," which will then lead to more frequent "I'm sorry" confessions.

Make the Toyota Production System a Pillar of the Management of the Entity

When a new president or CEO comes to the local entity, all the directors and employees are thinking, "I wonder what kind of person will come. I hope he or she is nice." They are both excited and a little nervous about who will show up. At a very early stage, please be very direct and clear in stating, "We will make the Toyota Production System a key pillar of management." Make sure that the people you are talking to see and feel your passion, your resoluteness, and your drive to do this.

Many books on the Toyota Production System or Lean system have been published, and many companies have had Lean consultants come in and give training. Most likely, your people who are involved in production have read more books than the Japanese and are more knowledgeable about the concepts. However, because of the many books and the many takes on the subject, many people are confused and do not really understand the principles. Also, even if outside consultants did come in, the training they provided may not have matched the needs of the business, so that the results were not as positive as had been expected.

One manager told me, "I read many books on the Toyota Production System. I even had experts come in and train us, but nothing got better. We are a make-to-order shop, and our lead time constraints are quite severe. When we get the job, we order the materials and parts, wait for them to come in, and then start production once they are all here. We have enough problems just getting things in on time, so concepts like heijunka, one-piece flow, and takt time are really hard to understand." These are obviously words from a very well-educated man who has taught himself a lot over the years.

Another big issue (and a big mistake, I may add) is that people think that the Toyota Production System is just a "production thing." There are many executives and managers in Japan who believe the same thing. When you say, "The Toyota Production System will be a pillar of management," many of the executives and managers will mistakenly think, "Our president will focus on production." You need to give the same speech in engineering and other specialist areas and give them actual examples so that they understand that this is for them as well.

Why does TPS become only a shop floor or production thing? I think it's because too many people say, "The foundation of TPS is doing 5S." For many days, people are forced to clean up their areas and do sorting and straightening. Every day they are told, "If you can't do 5S, you can't do TPS." After that, they learn how to make and fill out standard worksheets and do motion analysis. Many people think that using time and motion techniques to measure each step of a person's movements and get it closer to takt time is TPS, and that it will make the production areas more efficient.

People get frustrated because they never hear the words they read in the books—heijunka, takt time, downstream pull—from their sensei, so in the end they say, "I've had enough!" The CEO who hired the consultant, who was really looking forward to the results, now thinks, "This must only work in the automotive industry." Many people have this mistaken viewpoint.

The best way to get people to understand that this is not just a production thing but an "everybody thing" is to give good examples.

A good example is to describe all the hours spent on doing a month-end closing. All departments are affected by the process, so this is a great example. You could explain that we are now taking three weeks to close the books, but if, in the future, we could do it in one day, we could use real data to improve the processes; then elaborate on all the other benefits that would give.

When you are looking at numbers that are three weeks old, you have only one more week in the month to do anything about them, so any action that will be taken based on those numbers will happen in the next month. Also, if you are having monthly meetings about the numbers with your management staff and discussing what the problem is, it is the same as giving your well-paid management staff an undeserved holiday. There is no way for them to find out the reason for the change in defect rates for a product one month ago. However, if they don't say anything, it looks as if they are not taking this seriously, so they will offer different opinions. In Japan, we call this "clouding up the tea," which is something that people who don't know enough about the tea ceremony will do to make it look as if they are doing something purposeful and useful. We are now basically using our valuable time "clouding up the tea."

This kind of meeting is the definition of muda and nothing else. "Let's use fresh numbers and take meaningful action. If we don't, we won't be able to keep up with the world around us!" Please help them understand how important this concept is.

When it comes to design or engineering, they have a deadline for the start of production that they need to meet; they base their schedule on that and figure out how many resources (people) they need. If they don't have enough resources, they ask HR for more people. Remember, the job of the manager is to create flow. It's the same in engineering. Say, "Think of how you can make the job of your employees easier. The role of the manager is to improve the job and to fix the problems so that extra resources are not needed." The goal is lead-time reduction through incorporating flow. When the staff divisions and engineering get on board, then we have a companywide tenet of "making the Toyota Production System our management pillar" becoming a reality. At the same time, you should announce that you will do this with your suppliers as well. This message will get to your suppliers right away, since the grapevine works extremely well.

Be Proactive in Encouraging the Toyota Production System Inside and Outside Your Company

It starts with making the structure for the promotion of the Toyota Production System. This does not mean creating a separate "Lean office," but rather including all members of management as members. Explain the four stages of things and start by reducing the waiting time. Decide on a model line and start by moving toward flow. I don't think "reducing waiting" is on the first floor of our cultural building in most cases. (However, if people are being paid for piecework or by yield, then it's best not to touch those areas.) Make a finished goods store and use kanbans to prevent the risk of overproduction.

You should do this the same way Ohno did it. Ask each supervisor how much finished goods inventory she needs in order to manage the area, and then give her as many kanbans as she needs in order to feel secure. Even if you think the supervisor is saying that she needs more than she really does, don't argue about that at this moment.

After the supervisor is feeling secure, you can tell her, "Please find out the reasons for waiting and reduce the amount of the finished goods inventory a little bit at a time. The finished goods amount you have now reflects the ability of your line. Please use and increase your strengths and skill to decrease this amount." If you say it this way and ask the supervisor to improve, then she will be motivated to do so. She will know that the president is interested in her finished goods amount. If it goes down, she will be praised, and if it goes up, we will find out the reason and encourage her to reduce it.

A typical foreign operation is smaller in scale, so you can get directly involved with your own eyes and feelings. People will recognize that the president wants to work with them to make the lines better. It will create a nice, friendly atmosphere, and the employees will enjoy the journey of making improvements.

Next, it will be time to work with the suppliers, but you will now have a line that you can show them. That's what the model line is for. It will be effective only if you can create a model line that people in that country could not see elsewhere. Have your production engineering staff research what is out there and create the new line. Of course, a downstream pull/replenishment line would be the best type. If the function is assembly, it needs to be a one-piece-flow kitted line. It should be a dedicated line with low-cost automation incorporated in it.

Choose a Local Manager for Working with Suppliers

Now we are ready to work with our suppliers. Choose one local manager for this responsibility so that all the local suppliers will learn it the same way. A lot of times, you will be dealing with another company that is a wholly owned subsidiary of a Japanese company. In such a case, you may think that the teacher should be a Japanese person, but you will get a better mid- to long-term result if you do the deployment through your local manager. Just because the company is Japanese doesn't mean that the employees learned things the correct way.

There are countless Toyota Production System senseis in Japan. A lot of people have been trained by these teachers, who were under pressure to show results quickly. There is a strong likelihood that people who were taught this way will break the rules of engagement to show a quick result, which will keep continuing this unhelpful cycle.

We want to take a local manager to teach a local supplier who hasn't been touched yet. The local manager has hardly any experience teaching the Toyota method, so he will be able to teach only the foundational aspects and stick to them. This is actually a very good thing.

The supplier would much rather have a person who teaches the foundational things and starts from zero than a Japanese manager who *sort of* knows how to teach. This way, both your supplier and your employee will have a valuable growing experience.

Please tell the manager who will be the trainer not to "just look for efficiencies." This is something that we need to teach all our managers when they are dealing with suppliers. The reason we are teaching our suppliers is not to achieve short-term price reductions and reduce our cost, but to really ensure that they grow in the long term. When someone is focusing just on short-term price reductions, you may actually do the supplier more harm than good.

So whom should you choose to be your local trainer? It should be one of your current managers who has taken an interest in, thinks hard about, and has seriously applied herself to implementing the Toyota method. Obviously you have to be watching your managers in their day-to-day work to make this judgment about them.

If possible, it will be great if they can speak Japanese (the language of your headquarters). Many times, if a person knows enough to train, he already has some knowledge of Japanese. However, the Toyota method is quite famous nowadays, and people may have a lot of knowledge of it, but not be able to speak Japanese. Make them learn Japanese, as they will be the ones who will be your right-hand men. Think of them as one day taking over the position of the factory manager.

The reason why we insist on using only one person is that if we have multiple trainers, there will be differences in the style and content of training, which may cause confusion. The best way to operate is to have one person train many other trainers. In Japan, there is still this feeling of safety: "I can train the person under me." What I mean is that concepts and institutions like lifelong work, seniority-based systems, company labor unions, and promoting from within are in place, so that the person whom you teach won't become your boss. This is where the basis of "feel safe to teach" comes from. In Japan, not many people think, "If I teach this person, will he be promoted over me?"

In countries other than Japan, these employment norms and the concept of growing your employees don't really exist, so you need to be really careful that you don't promote the student over her teacher.

As I mentioned in a previous chapter, the Toyota system is very dependent on having supervisors who can take charge of the operations and can be trusted to deal with emergencies and problems instead of the manager. In other words, growing your subordinates is an absolutely essential element of the Toyota Production System. Because of this, when you choose the local trainer for your suppliers or when people are being promoted, be careful to keep the teacher/student relationship in place. This is one test to see whether people will understand and accept this aspect of Japanese culture. Try to find out what "floor of the building" this idea will be on for the local people.

Another thing you will have to watch out for is that once word gets around that "this person is a great employee," other companies will try to take that employee that you have spent so much time developing away from you and have him work for them. If that person is really going to be the future leader, then you need to put him in a high enough managerial position to keep him; however, even that isn't a fail-safe method. You may have the experience that you trusted someone and even put him in what you thought was a high enough position to keep him, but he still resigned from your company. When that happens, put a smile on your face and send him off. You have developed a good person who will do a good service to his country.

How to Deploy the Toyota Production System in Suppliers

The purpose for teaching and deploying the Toyota Production System to your suppliers is to

1. See how seriously management takes production and operations.
2. Determine the suppliers' level of expertise in making good products.
3. Determine whether this is an entity that can be trusted to be a key supplier.
4. Give the supplier a way to continuously increase its performance.

Having said that, it's really hard to understand the first three points with just a few meetings and a couple of visits to the supplier's shop floor.

The best way to do this is to have your supplier decide on a model line that it wants to do TPS on and then have it present the current situation of that line to you. During that presentation, the supplier's level of understanding and what it thinks the issues are will be obvious. Don't just listen to the presentation; go to the actual area (gemba) and see for yourself. Check the improvement activities that are going on, the management, and the support staff, such as engineering. If you go to the actual area, the truth will become clear. If you keep "the four states of things" mentioned in Chapter 2 in mind, then you won't be deceived by nice presentations.

The starting point is to understand the level of the supplier you will be teaching and helping. That is because you need to adjust your teaching style to meet the level of the people you are working with. Please make sure that your trainers don't ignore the people they are training and just give them "the standard package."

As I mentioned before, there are many people who believe that the Toyota Production System starts with implementing 2S (Sort and Straighten; 5S is Sort, Straighten, Sweep, Standardize, and Self-Discipline), so you need to teach them the following five things:

1. Ohno's teachings
2. The role of top management, managers, and supervisors
3. The kind of management needed to be successful with the Toyota Production System
4. The four stages of things
5. The downstream pull/replenishment system

Please make sure that the top management understands these principles very well to begin with. Of course, many people immediately forget what they have just heard. That's OK; they will learn more as you continue to work with them. The main thing is that by teaching everyone first, they can remember that the Toyota Production System will apply to them directly as management.

Top Management Must Visit and Coach Suppliers at Least Three Times a Year

The trainer for the suppliers should be in charge of several companies and should visit them about once a week. That time should be spent listening to what they are having problems with or what they don't understand. The trainers should report this to the top (you), get instructions on how to deal with the issue, and deploy the solution at the supplier site accordingly.

In order to verify how things are progressing, the top person needs to go with the trainer and do a joint training session about once every two months. If the supplier realizes that the customer's top person (you) is serious about kaizen and is coming once every couple of months, the top person at the supplier will start thinking, "We need to increase the speed of improvement," or, "Next time we'll show this or that." This kind of positive mindset makes kaizen fun and meaningful.

Unfortunately, there will always be suppliers who do not enjoy having their customers come over and who will do the bare minimum necessary to "get a pass." This kind of negative attitude will not bring about good results, so your job is to get these suppliers to see that kaizen is fun and meaningful. Give them a good experience so that they will want to do more.

The other reason the top person should visit the suppliers is to see how her company looks and does business from the suppliers' point of view.

- How are we training them?
- Are we having them do the same work twice—once for us as the local customer and once for headquarters?
- Are our audits too strict?
- Are our incoming quality checks, such as visual inspection, too strict?
- Is their on-time delivery rate good?
- Are we making the price higher for ourselves because we want to avoid doing some work?

These kinds of things are best checked at the source.

When you come back, you can talk to the various departments that are involved in the issues you saw at the supplier, and ask them to find out more on the topic. If this starts happening regularly, some departments may start looking at their own work and fix the issues that are not right themselves without waiting for you to tell them to do so.

Even though your suppliers were going along with you at first because they had to and not because they wanted to, this attitude will change when they see issues that were bothering them getting fixed. They will give more power to the improvement activities and will start coming up with ideas of their own. In fact, they will actually start looking forward to your next visit!

You can get a lot clearer and truer picture of your company from the supplier's point of view than from your desk.

The Factory Must Be Run by Local Management, Starting with the Factory Manager and All the Way Down

This is going to be hard to do if you're just starting up operations in that country, but if your company has been there for 10 years and the Toyota Production System is moving along, then I highly recommend that you make the factory manager and all the managers in production local people.

I've seen many Western companies where the local people don't have much opportunity for promotion and where the management team comes from other companies. It seems that the HR policy is to control costs, and if people want a promotion, they need to change companies. Even in Japan, if the headquarters are overseas, this seems to be the practice. This may be standard practice for overseas companies, but Japanese companies should not copy this way of thinking.

OK, back to making management local people—someone who has come from Japan and is working in production actually has a lot of work to do. That work includes not only all the work that must be done locally, but also a lot of things that have to be done with the home country office, such as auditing, reporting, and generating ideas and requests. This alone is likely to consume most of the time available. Therefore, if the manager is Japanese, even if the local people have improvement ideas, there will be many occasions when the manager just can't give those ideas the attention they deserve. If this situation continues, it will negatively affect the relationships with the locals.

The fastest and most effective way of getting people to experience the joy of kaizen and to take responsibility for its implementation is to make all the managers, including the factory manager, local people.

The Japanese person who was the production manager up to now can be moved to production engineering and be made responsible for seeing through the improvement ideas generated from the gemba. If he feels that an improvement idea doesn't go far enough, he can explain this to the production people and have them improve on the idea themselves.

You never know, you may discover that your people have within them a tremendous talent for improving things. There is no feeling of accomplishment for doing a job when someone was telling you, "Do this. Do that." It is imperative that you give over control if you want people to get a feeling of accomplishment.

Localizing management also creates a nice atmosphere in operations. If the plant manager is local and those on the managerial staff are all local, many people will feel, "We can't let our factory manager down; we can't allow bad numbers to come from our plant; let's improve more." This will make the whole place feel like one team, and we will start seeing ripples of improvement going through the work areas.

A lot of times we see a nice improvement in the relationship between the Japanese management and local staff members when management is localized. Even though there is no longer the boss-subordinate relationship, the local manager will still want to discuss issues with the Japanese management.

The conversation is a lot more honest and fruitful without the hierarchical relationship that was there before.

No matter what, in the long term we have to make people responsible, so keep preparing yourself to be ready to do this and look for an opportune time.

Just turning over authority and responsibility will not work well, however. You especially want to be careful that you don't go back to the old days in Japan, where one couldn't say anything to production or didn't know what was going on.

Give responsibility, make and grow managers who can be responsible, and openly share issues and problems. Keep these three things in mind and keep working on the company's management structure.

Make Japanese the Official Company Language

There is another important aspect to localizing the management. Because this is a Japanese company, information related to part design, kaizen, production engineering, finance, production control, and scheduling is all in Japanese—the same language that the home office uses. (*To the reader: yes, I'm saying that if you make Japanese the official company language, you can localize management more easily. Please follow along for the reasoning and the translator Brad Schmidt's comments afterward.*)

You can cut down on the expense of having to send Japanese people to the local company and instead give the people in the local company a lot more opportunities to visit Japan. During these times, if they can visit the Japanese operations and hear things, their eyes and ears will be opened a lot more. Kaizen activity just got more power.

There is a lot of Japanese culture embedded in the Toyota Production System. Just looking at the hiring and promotion policy, we have nice words such as "develop your subordinates," "teamwork," "giving and taking help," and "feeling and saying 'sorry.'" You can say, "Many of these concepts cannot be said in another language, so we want you to study Japanese."

An expatriate may stay as long as six years, but she will eventually leave, and another person who doesn't understand the local language will come. If you are going back and forth by translating the local language into English and then from English into Japanese, any child who's ever played the telephone game can tell you how well this will work out. So what do people do? The Japanese just stick together and do everything by themselves.

If the local management can learn how to speak Japanese, not only will the Toyota Production System and kaizen become more effective, but also we can have a local site that has fast response and that can thrive within the overall company.

Brad's comment: *Obviously Mr. Harada is not recommending that everyone in the world who wants to do TPS learn to speak Japanese (although I am sure he would be happy to see that). The point here is the need for clear communication between the head office and the overseas plant. If a person does not speak the language of the head office, then communication will suffer, as will that person's career opportunities. Many of the concepts that are called "Japanese" are actually, in fact, quite biblical, meaning that there is a great foundation for them in Western culture. One concept that always works is to find the strength of that culture and use it to further the TPS deployment.*

Become an Executive Who People Can Trust. Respect Others and They Will Trust You

There are many things in the Toyota Production System that are quickly understood if they are explained properly. There are, however, many things that will change the way work is done, and it is hard for people to truly buy into and be supportive of them because of the resistance to change. To deal with this, in Japan we have often forced things through by saying, "Just do it first—you'll understand once you try it." In other words, we don't explain things; just saying "do it" is the norm here.

If one were to ask these teachers to explain, they would normally just talk about their experience and how their work changed. That's nice, but it is not a logical explanation—in fact, there are very few people who really understand the logic behind all of this, so we end up with, "Just do it. You'll get it if you try."

For your information, this method will not be successful overseas. You will also lose trust, and, even worse, people will think you are forcing things on them without giving them a chance to understand. If you were able to explain things, then people would think, "This person is too logical and leaves no room for dissent. He probably thinks that he is smart and we are stupid. There is no warmth coming from him." This also won't be effective.

How do you explain things like the following in an easy way?

1. Why can't we make one batch and transport the whole group together?
2. Wouldn't it be better to keep safety stock just in case the machine goes down? That way the line will not stop.
3. Why can't we work sitting down? It's less tiring this way.
4. Why must we make only one at a time?

If we were to go to the production area right away and say, "Change this area in such-and-such a manner," maybe the people will change it and it will look different, but they won't understand why things are being done that way.

The first step is to get the local directors, managers, and overseas staff to form a Toyota Production System Promotion Committee. The first few steps are key, so you need to spend time in a classroom setting training these people. Give them a summary and say, "These are the key points." Give them actual examples and explain why this system is different from the method that they are currently using. Explain what we want to change the method to and why.

I think the four stages of things as outlined in Chapter 2 is foundational and is very easy for most people to understand, so I recommend starting there. Start by asking, "How can we reduce the number of things that are sitting around?" Take questions, and always talk about specific ways of doing it.

After you have talked about the foundational aspects, say, "We will do one thing at a time and manually forward the work to the next area." "The finished goods will be put in a box one by one—different parts in different boxes." People will learn a lot better if they have to explain it (Brad's comment), so have the managers make materials or examples that they can use when they explain to their subordinates how this applies to them. Then have each department hold an introduction and explanation session with its employees.

When questions come up during the explanation sessions, make sure you bring them back to the Toyota Production System Promotion Committee and do a Q&A with all the managers. All the leaders need to understand what people are worried or apprehensive about and what will happen next. It will also be easier for them to discuss a third party's issues than to discuss their own, as many managers may be feeling the same way (Brad's comment). They all need to be thinking in terms of the same principles. Every time they get a question that they can't answer, have them bring it to the committee. Slow but steady should be the key idea.

When doing the Q&A in the committee, don't be in a hurry to give the answer. Sometimes the way you answer a question in Japan will not work or will be counterproductive in another country. Have the locals answer the question, and if their answer is different from yours, have them explain the reasons for their answer. You may find that there is a different kind of thinking in your country (Japan) and theirs, and if you are astute enough, you may even discover which floor of the building we are talking about. What you must definitely not say is, "The work that people have done up to now is muda, or waste." You also must not use a good old favorite, "You are moving, not working" (in Japanese, this is a play on words involving the characters *move* and *work*), or say anything that makes it seem as if what people have been doing up to now has been meaningless. Even though you may feel that something is obvious, the person who is hearing it for the first time won't change course unless she gets a proper explanation.

If you are to be able to explain things properly, you need to be asking yourself these questions before you fly overseas. See if you are convinced and why. You have many people around you with experience, so use them and ask them questions. You will meet people who can actually give a good explanation, and they will become your partners. There will always be some "deep thinkers" out there, so find those people who can help you make sense of this. Also, a great habit to get into is to ask "why, why" for everything—even things that are on the news.

If you are too verbose in your explanations, then your message will get lost in the translation, and pretty soon no one will know what you are talking about. A good explanation is, "We can do one-piece flow because we will develop the production bench strength," or "We don't need to make things in a batch because we will have the ability to do one-piece flow." Another is, "Let's make a profitable company together by reducing the parts sitting around by doing kaizen." Appreciate the hard work that the locals have given so far and paint a picture of success for their careers in the company as they grow and develop their skills so that they can see that their future is with the company.

One thing that will be met with resistance no matter how you say it is trying to make sitting-down work into standing-up work. This is one thing that you should not attempt to change at the start. If you force people to work standing up, you will lose their trust, and they will not understand why you are doing this—that it is the first step to their becoming more mobile so that they can learn new skills and processes, handle multiple processes, and help one another out. If you force them to stand up, there will be less of a cooperative spirit to learn different skills, and they will tend to resist pretty much everything you suggest.

Therefore, start with the areas that are cooperative. Once more and more areas are doing kaizen, the other areas will start to feel that they need to do something as well. People will start to feel, "We need to flow our work, because otherwise we'll look bad compared to the rest of the company," and multiprocess handling and standing work will be a lot easier to introduce. There are actually a lot of things that time itself will solve.

Don't skimp on the time spent answering questions—not just TPS questions, but all questions. Often the locals are asking you on behalf of everyone, so for every question, make sure that the person who is asking understands the answer well enough to explain it to her fellow workers. This is especially true for any questions from the union shop stewards.

If you keep the people behind the questioner in mind and you explain in a way that they understand, the local people will feel that they are respected. That will lead them to trust you. If you do not show respect, you can't earn trust. Answering questions in a respectful way is a great chance to create harmony.

This would be my advice on how to deploy the Toyota Production System overseas.

AFTERWORD

To Those Top Managers Who Are Thinking of Applying the Toyota Principles to Make a Wonderful Operation

Takehiko Harada

Looking back at the last 42 years of my life, starting with my joining Toyota, then being head of the factory engineering department in the Honsha plant, then becoming the acting CEO of Toyota's Taiwan Motors, and finally being the president of Chuo Spring Ltd., I see myself as following Ohno's teachings faithfully. For the last 10 years, I have been using the Toyota Production System as a pillar of management and have been a missionary in telling people how wonderful it can be when one applies TPS to one's operations. Even though I am just one person, weak and with faults, because of the greatness of the Toyota Production System, I have supported and witnessed people creating motivating workplaces. Because of this, I truly have no regrets in my corporate life. I am just grateful to people like Mr. Ohno and my various teachers, who gave me this wonderful gift.

I wrote this book to let people know that there is another way of doing things, one that gives purpose to work and also increases the number of smiles in the workforce.

I want top managers to deploy this system in their operations to allow people to work to their full potential and give much more value than ever before, thus enabling them to thrive in a competitive environment. Because of this, I have decided to write about how to deploy the Toyota Production System effectively.

If you want a successful deployment, then it is imperative that you value the concept of "all of us doing this together, helping one another out, and doing it at the same pace." This means that you will have to take the time to explain to people what will happen, decide roles and responsibilities, and be patient with one another.

We all understand the desire to get results fast, but when we say, "We want to deploy the Toyota Production System," that often means, "We will have to change parts of our corporate culture that have taken years to build." It's going to take a lot of effort and time to change that, so I suggest that you relax and, at first, don't stress yourself too much about the speed of deployment.

It is possible to create the appearance of TPS deployment fast, but the results will be short-lived. In an organization, there are principles and structure. There are rules, the operations follow the established structure, and the managers are involved in the different facets. In the same way, in the Toyota Production System, there are principles and a structure, and there is a need to establish that structure and the associated rules in the workplace. (Production lines and reorder points are good examples of this structure.)

In some areas, this will go smoothly because of good management. Others will struggle because of a lack of understanding. Whenever things start going wrong, people start asking the question, "Are we really doing the right thing?" and then the old culture rears its head to destroy the new culture that is being created.

That's why I mentioned "all of us doing this together, helping one another out, and doing it at the same pace." Changing the culture is going to be a huge task that everyone has to work hard at and be involved in.

One of the best ways to get everyone to buy in is to say, "We will do this by ourselves." I think this is the key to success. It's not as if we were in the days of Ohno, when no one was sure what she was trying to do or what the results would be. Nowadays, we can explain to people what kind of results we will get, and we can be pretty sure about it, too.

When the deployment runs into a wall and no one knows what to do next, that is the time to bring the whole management team together and decide on a road forward. Try it out, discuss how it went, think a bit more, and try again. Also, there are lots of books on the Toyota method out there, so I would encourage the use of them as well.

It will take a bit of trial and error, but I can guarantee that the bench strength developed during this process will be of great value to the company in the future. Keep explaining the logic to the supervisors and managers so that when results are realized, people understand why. It is, after all, your company, so take the necessary time and advance it at a pace that is sustainable.

The first step should be to focus on the four stages of things. Find out why the inventory is necessary and what purpose the work in process is serving, then reduce the amount of things that are waiting around. If frequent machine breakdowns are the problem, then focus on the machine and reduce the stoppages. If the quality is unstable, then repair the equipment and standardize the workers' processes to reduce the variability. If people are holding inventory because they are afraid of running out of parts, then talk with the leader of the area and decide how many parts should be held. As the ability of the area improves, the inventory can be reduced accordingly. Focus on this foundation. Keep reducing the amount of things waiting around and get closer to flow.

Once the amount of things that are waiting is reduced, this will mean that you have less time to solve problems that occur in everyday operations. Problems will appear faster, and also will affect other areas faster. This is actually your first result. Remember the words, "The manager's job is to create the environment where flow can happen." Many things in the company will now speed up, but this is just the beginning.

None of us wanted to do this to stop the line, so make sure that you keep enough inventory between processes to reflect the capability of the area. Once you get enough strength, you can continue to reduce this amount. Congratulate people and keep working toward a line that can flow.

What is necessary when doing kaizen is flexible thinking, honest effort, and the smiles of the people who are actually doing the improvement work. There will be no smiles present when people are forced to do this. The only thing present will be a lot of sighing. I have said this many times, but kaizen will not take root unless it is fun and meaningful. It's a great feeling when people are helping one another and coming together at areas that need more work to get them up to speed.

For me, the first step is getting to flow. Choosing flow gets production engineering involved. The work area has an active, happy atmosphere. People come up with improvement ideas. It is great when you start getting more team members on the kaizen team. In the end, you'll even get the design engineers involved and make it a whole company effort.

Once you get production engineering involved and make a one-piece-flow line, then you can make a store to hold the finished goods for that line and start with a downstream pull system. This is going to be very different from before, as the production instructions will come from the process after yours. Once this happens, you can bring out the champagne bottles. The ship is now ready to sail!

The standard out there seems to be, "You need to start with the 5S (Sort, Straighten, Sweep, Standardize, and Self-Discipline) when deploying the Toyota Production System." The interesting thing, though, is that when you follow the steps just outlined, the area somehow gets clean, it seems, all by itself. This is because there's been a change in people's minds and hearts.

Choose to make yours the method that takes people's natural tendencies and emotions into consideration, resulting in continuous and smile-filled improvements.

A heartfelt thanks to everyone's effort who made the publication of this book possible. It is truly appreciated.

Brad Schmidt

It has been a pleasure translating Mr. Harada's book, but an even greater pleasure knowing him and enjoying his friendship.

I have been a Lean consultant since 1998, and this book has helped me logically see what I have just emotionally experienced.

I want to express my thanks to the Makoto Japan team (DJ Duarte, Geno Johnston, and Sanja Tripkovic) for their support in allowing me to take the time to finish this book.

Finally, most of all, I want to thank Toshiko Narusawa, who introduced me to Mr. Harada, encouraged me to translate the book, and helped me to gain a deeper understanding of the principles discussed here. She has been a true friend and a reference for understanding the history behind Lean.

INDEX

ABOUT THE AUTHOR

Takehiko Harada

Joined Toyota Motor Corporation in 1968 in the machine department.

Learned the Toyota Production System (TPS) by doing it. Experience within Toyota includes machine department head, project general manager of the Operations Management Consulting Division (Toyota's TPS deployment group), and head of engineering works.

Became the president of Toyota's Taiwan Operations in 1999.

Became a director of Toyota Motor Corporation in 2000.

Became president of Chuo Spring, an automotive parts manufacturer, in 2005.

Retired in 2010. Currently is tirelessly showing company leaders how to use TPS to create great working environments, rather than using it to garner profits at the expense of the employees. His dry sense of humor and ability to link TPS with management behavior and a more profitable operation makes him a popluar speaker in Japan.

Takehiko currently resides in Toyota City, Japan.

Brad Schmidt, Makoto Investments

Brad was born and grew up in Japan and has worked as an interpreter for Japanese consultants throughout the world. His experience with individuals who worked directly with Ohno has given him unique insights into the concepts, their applications, and effective ways to implement change.

In 1998, Brad cofounded Gemba Research, a Lean consulting company in Seattle, and worked as a Lean deployment consultant in the United States and Europe.

In 2004, he established Makoto Investments in Tokyo, Japan, to consult with Japanese customers and to focus on the Japan Lean Experience, a benchmarking study tour to see different ways of implementing Lean. Brad and the participants then create a customized Lean deployment program that is effective because it is in accord with the organization's strengths.

Brad is one of the few Lean consultants who work with both Japanese and Western companies and is fluent in both English and Japanese.

He is currently working with a select few companies deploying Lean throughout their value streams, including Lean in R&D and headquarters functions—areas that are generally almost untouched by Lean.

Brad's focus is on training people and creating environments in which Lean activities take place naturally and the individual activities lead to real performance improvement.

Brad lives with his wife and two children in Tokyo, Japan.

CPSIA information can be obtained
at www.ICGtesting.com
Printed in the USA
LVOW10*0325020218
564951LV00002B/8/P